It's unfortunate that most books on [...] one extreme or the other. Some argue th[...] complete healing in the present age, while others are so skeptical of claims to healing that they virtually deny that any occur. This excellent and insightful book by Stephen Seamands is a much-needed corrective to both extremes. It is thoroughly biblical, pastorally sensitive, and does an excellent job of tethering the healing ministry of Jesus to the kingdom of God and the already/not yet of life in the present age. Seamands provides us with no easy, simplistic answers and does not avoid the mystery of why so many for whom we pray are not healed. And he does this in a way that fills the reader with expectancy each time hands are laid on the sick and prayer for their healing is taken to the throne of grace. If you're still looking for a book on healing, stop. Get this one. You won't be disappointed.

SAM STORMS, PhD, Enjoying God Ministries

When Steve Seamands talks about healing, he is speaking from decades of Spirit-led reflection, academic rigor, hands-on practice, and convincing proof that Jesus is still in the healing business. That's why I knew, as soon as I opened to the table of contents, that this book would benefit not only me but my whole congregation. I want everyone to use this book to build a vital healing ministry rooted in the love of God. What a gift to the body of Christ.

CAROLYN MOORE, lead pastor of Mosaic
Church and author of *When Women Lead*

I highly recommend Stephen Seamands, *Follow the Healer: Biblical and Theological Foundations for Healing Ministry*. It is not only solid biblically and theologically, but it also offers wisdom pastorally. I enjoyed reading it and was encouraged by its wisdom and insight.

DR. RANDY CLARK, president of Global Awakening Theological
Seminary and creator of the Christian Healing Certification
Program, author of *Power to Heal*; *Authority to Heal*; *The Healing
Breakthrough*; *The Essential Guide to Healing*; and *Anointed to Heal*

Follow the Healer is a compelling and accessible exploration of the healing ministry of Jesus Christ. Christ healed those who were broken in body and soul and still heals today! It is the love and compassion of God then and now that moves his heart to heal. God longs to restore his image in a fractured humanity. This is the message of his kingdom. Dr. Seamands expounds on the various ways in which God still heals today that are both supernatural and natural. Christ invites the church to participate in his healing ministry through the power and authority of the Holy Spirit. Though he presents the case of healing in a clear, concise, and convincing way, Seamands recognizes the complexity and even mystery of healing. Why and how are some healed and others not? The author is not afraid to face the dilemma and offers honest and careful guidance and assurance for those grappling with this mystery. Overall, *Follow the Healer* is a balanced, approachable, compassionate, and scriptural call to better understand and minister God's healing to a hurting world that desperately needs it.

> **PETER J. BELLINI**, Professor of Church Renewal and Evangelization in the Heisel Chair, United Theological Seminary, Dayton, Ohio

Follow the Healer answers the questions you've been wondering about healing and healing ministry. Is it biblical, practical, and experiential and comes from Dr. Steve Seamands's thirty years of involvement in healing prayer ministry with wounded and broken people. This book provides a Christocentric manual for this vital priority of the Christian faith and is a must read for anyone desiring to understand and implement healing ministry from a biblical, balanced, and holistic approach. Seamands addresses our critical questions about healing and healing ministry from the perspective of a practitioner, pastor, and theologian. *Follow the Healer* is one of the best books I've read to both better understand the priority of healing in Jesus's ministry and our responsibility to live into this priority today.

> **MATTHEW WHITEHEAD**, bishop of the Free Methodist Church, USA

Jesus is the Healer, follow him! Dr. Seamands writes a very accessible and helpful book on healing ministry. I appreciated his sound biblical approach to the topic and his stories. I was deeply touched by the love and humility that comes through the book and his chapters on suffering and mystery. I plan to use his book in my healing classes in the future.

Knowing Steven Seamands and having read his previous books, I knew *Follow the Healer* would be biblically grounded, theologically sound, and completely balanced. What I did not anticipate was the degree to which I would be personally impacted by the Holy Spirit. I felt the presence of the living Christ as I read, and I was repeatedly enveloped in the compassionate love of the Father. I experienced an episodic awakening, not simply to the ministry of healing, as important as that may be, but to the movement of the kingdom of God. Read this book and you will find your faith in Christ ignited and sense a holy invitation to follow Jesus in his healing ministry of restoring broken people, all to the glory of God.

FOLLOW
THE
HEALER

BIBLICAL
AND THEOLOGICAL
FOUNDATIONS
FOR HEALING
MINISTRY

FOLLOW
THE
HEALER

STEPHEN SEAMANDS

ZONDERVAN REFLECTIVE

Follow the Healer
Copyright © 2023 by Stephen A. Seamands

Requests for information should be addressed to:
Zondervan, *3900 Sparks Dr. SE, Grand Rapids, Michigan 49546*
Seedbed Publishing, *415 Bridge Street, Franklin, Tennessee 37064*

Zondervan titles may be purchased in bulk for educational, business, fundraising, or sales promotional use. For information, please email SpecialMarkets@Zondervan.com.

ISBN 978-0-310-15769-4 (audio)

Library of Congress Cataloging-in-Publication Data

Names: Seamands, Stephen A., 1949- author.
Title: Follow the healer : biblical and theological foundations for healing ministry / Stephen Seamands.
Description: Grand Rapids : Zondervan, 2023.
Identifiers: LCCN 2023009946 (print) | LCCN 2023009947 (ebook) | ISBN 9780310157670 (paperback) | ISBN 9780310157687 (ebook)
Subjects: LCSH: Healing x Religious aspects--Christianity. | BISAC: RELIGION / Christian Living / Prayer | RELIGION / Christian Living / Spiritual Growth
Classification: LCC BT732 .S423 2023 (print) | LCC BT732 (ebook) | DDC 234/.131—dc23/eng/20230422
LC record available at https://lccn.loc.gov/2023009946
LC ebook record available at https://lccn.loc.gov/2023009947

Cover design: Bruce Gore | Gore Studio, Inc.
Cover image: © José Luiz Bernardes Ribeiro / CC BY-SA 3.0
Interior design: Sara Colley

Printed in the United States of America

23 24 25 26 27 28 29 30 31 32 /TRM/ 14 13 12 11 10 9 8 7 6 5 4 3 2 1

To all those who through their friendship,
personal influence, example, and writings have
taught me about following the Healer:

Dan Allender, Neil Anderson, Randy Clark, Larry
Crabb, Andy Comiskey, Jack Deere, Don Demaray,
Chris Dunagan, Larry Eddings, Anne Haley, Tommy
Hays, Peg Hutchins, E. Stanley Jones, Charles Kraft,
Frank Lake, Brad Long, Martin Mallory, Francis and
Judith MacNutt, Russ Parker, Leanne Payne, Mark
Pierson, David Seamands, A. B. Simpson, Frank
Stanger, Myra Stradt, Cindy Strickler, Steve Stratton,
Paul Tournier, Terry Wardle, John and Charles Wesley,
Tom White, Smith Wigglesworth, and John Wimber

CONTENTS

FOREWORD

Let me introduce you to Dr. Steve Seamands. I first met Steve thirty years ago when I was a new seminary student. For several decades I have known him as a theology professor, mentor, pastor, and friend, and all of these various roles come together in Steve's long and faithful participation in the healing ministry of Jesus and the healing mission of his church. When I became the president and publisher of Seedbed, I began a campaign to enlist Steve to write the book you now hold in your hands.

Most of the books on healing ministry we read these days are trying to convince us that Jesus still heals people. This book assumes that's true. The point of this work is to resource the church with a practical theology of healing—to understand the full range of *how* Jesus heals and how we as his agents can participate in the ministry and mission of Jesus in and through our local churches for the sake of the world.

If you will, permit me to make a bold statement, and then share two quick stories and an invitation. First—my bold statement. *The church of Jesus Christ is the primary agency of healing in the world.*

And my first story. I will never forget the day the late Francis McNutt visited our seminary chapel. He came, in the tradition of Jesus, to teach, preach, and heal. Fr. McNutt, a Catholic priest, had given his life and ministry to participating in the healing ministry of Jesus. He began his message by asking a question, calling for a show of hands: *Who in this chapel has a memory from their childhood of being sick and their parents directly praying with and for them for healing?*

There were over four hundred people in the room, yet maybe only thirty hands went in the air. McNutt said he asked that question everywhere he had traveled and ministered for the past three decades, and the response here was slightly higher than the norm. He said that on average no more than 10 percent of people in church today have any memory of a parent praying for them when they were a sick child.

Here is story number two.

On March 11, 2020, the World Health Organization officially declared COVID-19 a global pandemic. A few days later, on March 15, the shutdown of all nonessential institutions began. And among the first of those major institutions to be shut down from normal operations were many Christian churches.

How is it that *the* central healing agency in the world was the first to shut down in the face of the worst disease the world had seen in generations? I believe it's the same reason less than 10 percent of children from Christian homes have any memory of a parent praying for them when they were sick. And it raises a question I have begun to ask doctors, nurses, and any other healthcare worker (including mental-health professionals) I encounter. Have you ever been identified, equipped, commissioned, or anointed by the church as a healer in the way of Jesus? Do you have any sense—regular, occasional, or otherwise— that you are being sent out by the church to carry out your vocation as a mission of healing in Jesus's name and authority? Has your church ever prayed with and for you as an agent of Jesus in any identifiable or designated way for the fulfillment of your vocation in the medical profession? Despite lots of prayers for God to guide the hands of the surgeons, I have yet to meet a health-care professional who has been set apart and prayed for in the body of believers as a healer in Jesus's name.

Thankfully, there remains widespread belief today that God heals. But there appears to be very little confidence the church of Jesus Christ has much to do with that healing. We are not facing a deficit of faith in the power of God to heal; we are confronting the absence of a practical theology of healing in the local church.

Here's the invitation. It's not to start a healing prayer group at your church—as good as that would be. My invitation is to plant this book, like a seed, into the soul of your own heart, into your hopes for your church and city. This book aims to raise up new generations of Christians to follow Jesus the Healer and so become healers in his name.

So here's to parents praying for sick children (and vice versa)—not as the last resort but as the first aid. Here's to our local-church altars being regularly filled with anyone and everyone who works in the health-care profession and industry for prayer, consecration, commissioning, and fresh anointing for their participation in the healing ministry of Jesus. Yes, here's to recovering the church as the central agency of healing in the world. And when the next global pandemic rolls around—and it will—may the church be ready to meet that moment in a way that reveals the Great Physician superintending the fully orbed, supernaturally engaged ministry of his church, blessing the world with healing.

J. D. WALT
sower-in-chief, Seedbed

ONE

PARTICIPATING IN THE HEALING MINISTRY OF JESUS

Healing played an essential part in Jesus's three-year earthly ministry. In fact, along with teaching and preaching, it was one of his three major activities. The Gospel of Matthew sums up Jesus's ministry in Galilee like this: "Jesus went through all the towns and villages, *teaching* in their synagogues, *proclaiming* the good news of the kingdom and *healing* every disease and sickness" (9:35, emphasis added; cf. 4:23–24).

Not only did Jesus heal, but he insisted that his disciples and followers heal as well. Sending them out two by two, he "gave them authority to drive out impure spirits and to heal every disease and sickness" (Matt. 10:1), and he commanded them to "heal the sick, raise the dead, cleanse those who have leprosy, drive out demons" (Matt. 10:8). And they did.

But what happened after Jesus died, rose, and ascended into heaven? Did his ministry of healing come to an abrupt end? Definitely not. It merely assumed a different shape. Now Jesus's healing ministry, like his preaching and teaching ministry, continues on earth through his body, the church.

Yet what exactly does that mean for us today? What is Christian healing ministry supposed to look like? How do we go about it? What forms and expressions should it take? Furthermore, how do we evaluate it? And how do we determine whether the healing ministry we are involved in is in keeping with what Jesus intended?

For more than thirty years, I have been involved in healing prayer ministry with broken, wounded people. To share my knowledge and experiences, I authored a book on emotional healing.[1] Later I began teaching a class on the theology and practice of healing at Asbury Theological Seminary. My experience has convinced me that in addition to the significant practical training and instruction we need in healing ministry, we also need biblical and theological foundations to undergird and inform our practice.

Simon Sinek has written a bestselling, influential book on leadership, in which he urges leaders to "Start with Why," because "If you don't know WHY, you can't know HOW."[2] I believe the same holds true for those of us involved in healing ministry. The how-tos are very important. But it's imperative to start with the why-tos because ultimately, whether we are aware of it or not, they will profoundly shape the how-tos. Many of the difficulties, disappointments, and distortions that occur in healing ministry stem from a failure to start with the why-tos. Thus, they are the focus of this book.

You may have had extensive experience in healing ministry or are just a beginner; you may be a pastor or lay leader who senses a growing need for healing ministry in your congregation. You may be a small group leader, a prayer minister, or someone who simply wants to learn more about healing in general. My desire is to present, clearly and accessibly, essential biblical and theological foundations on which you can build a ministry of healing regardless of your level of experience or interest. I intend to show you what a profound impact these why-tos can have on your practice of healing.

Let me be clear that this is a book on *Christian* healing, not healing in general. I am part of the Christian tribe— the pan-Wesleyan tribe (Anglican, Methodist, Holiness, Pentecostal, charismatic, Third Wave) that grew out of the ministry of John and Charles Wesley. Healing played an important part in their understanding of the Christian message. In fact, many of their insights and practices related to healing are relevant and applicable today. I will be mentioning some of these along the way. Yet although I write from a Wesleyan perspective, my primary concern is to encourage healing ministry among all Christians everywhere.

3

WHOSE MINISTRY IS IT?

But enough by way of introduction. Let's get started. I said that Jesus's healing ministry didn't end when he ascended into heaven; it merely assumed a different shape. His ministry of healing, like his ministry of teaching and preaching, continues through his followers, through his body, the church. But be sure to notice this: it's *his* ministry that continues.

The biblical and theological foundation I discuss in this chapter is so crucial and essential, yet so obvious, we often overlook it. Here it is: the healing ministry to which we are called is not primarily *our* ministry but *Christ's*. What we are called to do is to participate in the *ongoing* healing ministry of Jesus Christ.

Luke emphasized this at the very beginning of the book of Acts. In his first book (the Gospel of Luke) he said that he wrote about "all that Jesus *began to do and teach*" (Acts 1:1, emphasis added). Notice he didn't say "all that Jesus *did and taught*" as we might expect. That's because Luke was convinced that Jesus's ministry on earth didn't end when he ascended into heaven. In reality, it had only just begun. The reason Luke was writing this second book (Acts) was to tell the story of the *ongoing* ministry of Jesus through his apostles and his followers.

So this seemingly insignificant phrase—"All that Jesus began to do and teach"—is actually extremely significant. According to John Stott, it "sets Christianity apart from all other religions." These regard their founders, such as

4

Muhammad, Buddha, or Confucius, as having completed their ministries in their lifetimes. Luke, however, said "Jesus only began his."[3]

Jesus has been raised from the dead. He is now more alive than ever. And not only did his resurrection mean the resurrection of his body; it also meant the resurrection *of his ministry*. He has also ascended into heaven so that now, through the Holy Spirit, he is able to fill all times and places with his actual presence.[4]

By no means, then, has Jesus been put on the shelf. He is much more than our cheerleader in heaven, hoping we'll do ministry right. Jesus has his own resurrected, ascended ministry of teaching, preaching, and healing to do. And he intends to do it through us—his body, the church.

But never forget, Jesus is the chief actor in ministry. *We are called to participate in his ongoing ministry of healing, to join him in his ministry rather than asking him to help us carry out ours.* He is the healer—not us. Our job is to follow the Healer.

Because of our deep-seated tendency as fallen human beings to put ourselves at the center of everything, to make things about ourselves, we must be constantly reminded of this. So I'll say it again: healing ministry is not primarily your ministry. It's not about Jesus helping you as you minister to others; it's about you joining him as he continues his ministry of healing through you. After thirty plus years of involvement in healing prayer ministry, I am more convinced of this than ever. Yet how often I forget and still need to be reminded.

WHY THIS MATTERS SO MUCH

This foundational truth about healing ministry has profound practical implications. I'll tell you about four of them. First, it *shapes the way we pray* as we engage in healing ministry. As we prepare for healing ministry, we often pray "Lord, help me" prayers. For example, "Lord, they've asked me to pray with people who come forward to request prayer for healing during the Communion service this Sunday at church. Would you help me as I pray for them?"

To be sure, there's nothing wrong with "Lord, help me" prayers like that. There are many in the Bible, especially in the Psalms. But when you realize that it's more about you joining Jesus than him helping you, then it's better to pray, "Lord, *help yourself to* me. Lord, *use* me. You are here working. What do you want to say or do? Let me join you. Don't let me get in the way of what you are doing."

Someone once asked Mother Teresa the secret of her amazing, awe-inspiring ministry among the sick and dying in Calcutta. "I'm just a little pencil in God's hands," she immediately replied. "He does the thinking. He does the writing. He does everything and sometimes it is hard because it is a broken pencil, and He has to sharpen it a little more."[5]

Mother Teresa understood that her job was to be a pencil—and notice she said a *little*, not a big pencil. She was willing to be little enough. And she also understood that it was God's job to do the thinking and writing.

Like Mother Teresa, understanding whose ministry it is

shapes the way we pray in preparation for healing ministry. We find ourselves praying, "Lord, help yourself to me. Help me simply to be a little pencil. Dull and broken though I am, use me to accomplish your work through me."

Second, and perhaps most importantly, understanding whose ministry it is *relieves us of the burden of ministry.* For if, in fact, it's Christ's healing ministry, then ultimately he is the one who is responsible. It's his burden, not ours. We don't have to make it happen. He does. Our task is merely to *let* it happen.

We are prone to take the burden of ministry on ourselves, assuming it all depends on us. Whenever we do, we saddle ourselves with a heavy burden we were never designed to carry. Jesus's yoke is easy, and his burden is light (Matt. 11:30). Knowing that healing ministry is his burden, not ours, brings joy and rest to our souls (Matt. 11:29).

A Christian leader who was in a class I taught several years ago shared with me what a difference it made as she began to grasp this. Here's how she described what happened:

I work at a mental health hospital as a clinical counselor. In the past, my prayer, as I entered work, was always to ask Christ to lead me and guide me through my ministry, helping me to be a vehicle instead of a barrier. For one week I prayed instead that Christ would allow me to accompany him, asking him to fill me with the Holy Spirit and allow me to piggyback on his ministry.

It was the most exciting ministry with the most surprising results. The anxiety I usually experienced as I entered the building was gone. I was smiling and felt a power around me that felt unstoppable. My colleagues responded to me differently, often asking for guidance or consultations. And the clients prospered.

My days were filled with something bigger than I ever could have imagined. I liked coming to work. My journey became bigger than I am because it was bigger than I am. I was tagging alongside Jesus through the Holy Spirit. This outward journey was making an incredible difference in my own life and making an incredible difference in the lives of my clients.

The whole change led to a promotion for me to supervisor. My seven days has turned into an ongoing approach to ministry.

I certainly can't guarantee you a promotion, but I can guarantee that your load will be lighter, and you will be more fun to live with! Knowing whose ministry it is means knowing whose burden it is—Jesus's not ours. Ultimately, we are not the ones who are responsible. We don't have to lead or to heal. We just must follow the Leader and the Healer.

Third, understanding that healing is a participation in the ongoing healing ministry of Christ *increases our confidence and boldness as we minister.* Think of it this way: every time we enter a place to engage in healing prayer ministry with someone, we can rest assured that the risen Christ is there with us. Actually, he arrived there before we did and is waiting for us to join him.

The angel at the empty tomb on Easter morning told the women to tell the disciples, "He is going ahead of you into Galilee. There you will see him, just as he told you" (Mark 16:7). Something similar happens as we engage in the ministry of healing prayer. We learn to acknowledge the presence of the one who is already there.

In her wonderful book *The Healing Presence*, Leanne Payne captures this idea well:

> He it is who comes and heals. It is He who befriends the sinner, releases the captive, and heals the lame in mind and body. . . . We learn to practice the Presence of Jesus within (our bodies are temples of the Holy Spirit), without (He walks alongside us as Companion and Brother), and all around (He is high and lifted up, and we exalt Him as Sovereign God. And we ask Him to love the world through us. We learn to collaborate with Him. We do what we see Him doing . . . we simply trust in His Presence with us.[6]

Knowing that Jesus is present with us and will meet us also enables us to approach ministry with greater confidence—not in ourselves, but in who Jesus is and what he desires to do.

Years ago, when I had first begun to engage in healing

prayer, I was ministering to the wife of a seminary student. As I listened to her unpack the tangled, sordid story of her life, I felt overwhelmed. There was so much trauma, pain, and baggage, so many complicated problems and emotional issues to deal with, so many layers that needed healing. As a result, I found myself desperately praying, "Lord, I don't have a clue where to begin. But I know you do. You've been working in her life, and you're here now. Come now and reveal yourself and your presence in our midst."

I can't remember what I said, what questions I asked, or even if I said anything, but before I knew it, Jesus had answered my prayer. He came into the situation, revealed himself to her, and put his finger on the exact place where she needed to begin her healing journey. Forty-five minutes later, as she left my office, she was effusive in thanking me over and over for how much I had helped her.

After she had left, I sat there stunned and silent, shaking my head in awe at what had just transpired. "Lord," I asked, "how in the world did that happen? I didn't do anything!"

"Yes, you did," Jesus seemed to whisper. "You made yourself available to me. You invited me to come, and when I did, you didn't get in the way."

The key to fruitful healing prayer ministry is to be so open and available to the risen Christ that he is free to manifest himself as you listen and counsel and pray with people. Knowing it's his ministry in which we've been invited to participate increases our confidence and expectancy. He really does want to show up! So often, after praying with someone, I've come away thinking, *Jesus, our prayer team didn't know what we were doing today! But somehow we backed into doing exactly what was right. The way you revealed to us how to pray, the way you manifested your presence in our midst—you wanted that person to experience healing much more than we did!*

Fourth, understanding whose ministry it is *determines our primary calling.* Abiding in Christ, not healing ministry, is what matters most. As Jesus stressed in his parable of the vine and the branches (John 15:1–8), branches bear fruit only as they abide in the vine. "Those who abide in me and I in them bear much fruit, because apart from me you can do nothing" (v. 5 NRSV). When we make abiding in him our top priority, Jesus himself will come and dwell in us. And then he will accomplish his healing ministry through us.

Often when I am taking time in the morning to abide in Christ through prayer, devotional reading, and meditating on Scripture, I will find myself thinking about a healing prayer appointment I have with someone later in the day. When that happens, my natural tendency has been to pray, "Lord, help me as I meet with so-and-so. Give me your strategy for our time together. Do you have a word you want me to convey to them? Speak Lord, I'm listening now. Show me what you want me to do and say."

Most of the time I hear nothing. Instead of answering

my prayer, Jesus seems to say, "Steve, don't worry about that appointment right now. Just concentrate on me and your relationship with me. Abide in me. In fact, I really care more about that than anything you'll ever do for me, Steve. So dwell in me, worship me, and love me. Receive my love for you. Enter into the joy of my rest."

I've discovered that when I focus on that—when I make it more about abiding in Christ and less about asking for help concerning what lies ahead—then when I'm in the healing prayer session, he will have freer rein and will come and accomplish his healing work through me. As Paul expressed it so beautifully in his letter to the Colossians, "The secret is simply this: Christ in you! Yes, Christ in you bringing with him the hope of all glorious things to come" (Col. 1:27 PHILLIPS).

Abiding in Christ is our primary calling. And Jesus promised that if we abide in him, he will abide in us (John 15:4) and we will bear fruit (v. 5). This, of course, is why the various spiritual practices or disciplines, or "means of grace," as John Wesley liked to call them, are so vital and indispensable. As many and as varied as they are, they are all ways of abiding in Christ.

I trust you are beginning to realize why it matters so much that you understand whose ministry it is you are entering. Knowing that it's essentially Jesus's ministry and not ours shapes the way we pray, relieves us of the burden of ministry, increases our confidence in his healing presence, and determines our primary calling.

THE THREEFOLD PATTERN OF THE MINISTRY OF JESUS

The ministry of healing prayer truly is a coworking ministry where Jesus leads and we follow. We partner with him in his ongoing healing ministry today. What's more, as we follow the Healer, the three main movements in Christ's own earthly ministry provide us with a basic overarching pattern that defines and shapes our practice of healing.

The apostle Paul succinctly described these movements in Philippians 2:5–11. Most scholars agree that this is one of the most significant passages concerning the life and ministry of Jesus in the New Testament. The three movements the apostle described—incarnation, crucifixion, and resurrection—are so central to our faith that the major seasons of the church year—Advent, Lent, and Easter—revolve around them. They also provide an overarching pattern for us as we engage in the practice of healing prayer. For as Christ's ministry continues in the world today, it generally follows the same pattern now in the present—as it did then—in the past.

Let's consider the three movements Paul laid out in this passage and how these movements unfold in the context of healing ministry.

1. INCARNATION

Who, being in very nature God,
> *did not consider equality with God something to be*
> *used to his own advantage;*

rather, he made himself nothing
by taking the very nature of a servant,
being made in human likeness. (Phil. 2:6–7)

Paul said that Jesus, the eternal Son of God, emptied himself of his rightful claim to divinity. To identify with us fully in our humanity, he assumed a human body and experienced all our human limitations. He dwelt among us (John 1:14), sharing in our guilt and our suffering. He became Emmanuel—God with us—eyeball to eyeball, heart to heart.

As a result, through Christ's incarnation, the full extent of God's love and affirmation of humanity have been revealed. For by assuming the likeness of sinful flesh (Rom. 8:3) and joining himself to fallen humanity in the person of his Son, God was in effect declaring, "Though you are sinful and fallen, I choose not to reject or destroy you. I believe in you so much that I am becoming one of you. I am committed to you and will redeem you."

Through the incarnation, then, we learn of God's affirmation, of his resounding yes to humanity. And through the healing prayer minister, God desires to convey that affirmation to persons in need of healing. Jesus works through us to come alongside people, creating an atmosphere of trust and safety, and nurturing a relationship of love and acceptance.

Building a positive, heart-to-heart relational bridge between Jesus, ourselves, and the person provides the necessary context for healing ministry. Without this vital and essential first step, a deep work of healing will not happen. As Brad Long and Cindy Strickler rightly insist, "It all starts with a relationship between Jesus and the person. Without this relationship, all the love and power of God are impotent to heal the hurts hidden in the human heart."[7]

Taking time for people, engaging them in conversation, giving them eye contact, actively listening to them, offering them unconditional, nonjudgmental acceptance, expressing genuine empathy, letting them know we value them—these are building blocks in that indispensable relational bridge. Through us Jesus is saying, "I'm here beside you and I hear you. I love you and accept you; I value you and want to help."

2. CRUCIFIXION

> And being found in appearance as a man,
>   he humbled himself
>   by becoming obedient to death—
>   even death on a cross! (Phil. 2:8)

Jesus identified with the human condition all the way to the point of dying a shameful, gruesome, violent death on a cross. And according to the prophet Isaiah, he died on account of our sin. He was wounded for our transgressions and bruised for our iniquities. He bore our sufferings and infirmities, the guilt and curse of our sin (Isa. 53:3–5).

Moreover, through his death, the gravity of our sin is fully exposed. Our rebellion against God is so deep-seated and intense that we would kill God if we could. God's judgment on human sin—separation and death—is also clearly revealed at the cross.

In direct contrast to Christ's incarnation, which reveals God's yes to humanity, his crucifixion reveals God's no to human rebellion and sin. In his abandonment, when he cried out, "My God, my God, why have you forsaken me?" (Mark 15:34), Jesus himself experienced the depth and the force of that no, of God's condemnation of sinful, fallen humanity.

Through the ministry of healing prayer, Jesus also invites us to confront the reality and face the truth about the nos of sin and suffering we have personally experienced. Jesus won't heal those things that we insist on hiding from him. He insists that we confront the pain and embrace the suffering as he did in enduring the cross. Yet we will not have to walk that way alone, because Jesus himself promises to walk with us, no matter how painful or dark the path on the healing journey.

That path may include a number of difficult but necessary steps, such as breaking through denial, revisiting painful memories, owning our deep-seated anger, overcoming our fears, admitting our failures and guilt, letting go of comfortable protective strategies, grieving our losses, forgiving those who have wronged us, and even descending into depression. In healing prayer, as we walk with people, helping them slowly step into such dark places, Jesus walks with them and communicates his strength and his presence through us.

3. RESURRECTION

Therefore God exalted him to the highest place
and gave him the name that is above every name,
that at the name of Jesus every knee should bow . . .
and every tongue acknowledge that Jesus Christ is Lord,
to the glory of God the Father. (Phil. 2:9–11)

Jesus, who was condemned to die, has now been raised by God to new life and given a name above every name. God's love for fallen creation and humanity is therefore stronger than death. Through the miracle of resurrection, God heals and re-creates. The old has passed away, all things become new. Through Christ's resurrection, new creation springs forth.

Thus, God's will for the fallen world stands clearly revealed. He desires to heal his broken creation and make all things new. In the midst of the old world of decay and death, resurrection has dawned as a living reality in the present and as the promised future of a new heaven and a new earth (Rev. 21–22).

In the ministry of healing prayer, we often witness Christ's resurrection power being unleashed. Just as he appeared to the two men on the road to Emmaus (Luke 24:13–35), the risen Christ comes and meets us in profound ways. Physical and emotional and spiritual healing happens before our eyes. Breakthroughs occur. Healing light streams into dark places in our souls. Spiritual and emotional chains fall off. Broken hearts are mended. Demonic strongholds are broken. Deliverance comes to those who are bound. Strength to persevere is imparted. Fractured relationships are mended. Identity is established. Callings are discovered. Songs are released. Sorrow and sighing flee away (Isa. 35:10).

SUMMARY

In healing prayer, as we participate in the healing ministry of Jesus, we find these three movements ever unfolding and providing us a pattern for our ministry. That pattern is the same now as it was then: incarnation (affirmation), crucifixion (confrontation), and resurrection (new creation).

I mentioned the risen Christ's encounter with the two men on the road to Emmaus. Because it is such a vivid example of this threefold pattern, as I close this chapter I will briefly describe how it unfolded.

INCARNATION (AFFIRMATION)

Jesus came alongside the two downcast disciples and walked with them, though they failed to recognize him. He joined their conversation, and noticing their downcast faces, inquired about what happened to make them sad. He listened empathetically as they painfully recounted how their hopes had been dashed when Jesus of Nazareth, the man they were convinced was the Messiah, was crucified (Luke 24:15–24).

CRUCIFIXION (CONFRONTATION)

It may have been painful and unsettling, another blow to their already disappointed hearts, but Jesus found it necessary to confront them. He walked them through the Old Testament Scriptures and called into question their false expectations about the Messiah: "How foolish you are, and how slow of heart to believe. . . . Did not the Christ have to suffer these things and then enter his glory?" (Luke 24:25–26).

RESURRECTION (RE-CREATION)

Later, when they stopped to eat, there came that moment—in the breaking of the bread—when Jesus revealed himself to them: "Then their eyes were opened and they recognized him, and he disappeared from their sight" (Luke 24:31). In that instant, everything changed, and they exclaimed, "Were not our hearts burning with us while he talked with us on the road?" (v. 32). Immediately they turned around and walked back to Jerusalem to tell the disciples, "It is true! The Lord has risen." And they "told what had happened on the way" (vv. 34–35).

They rushed back to tell others of their encounter with the risen Christ. As a result, their *burdened* hearts became *burning* hearts—burning hearts that then became *bold* hearts.

In healing prayer ministry, Jesus invites us to come alongside him as he comes alongside those who are hurting to affirm them, confront them, and restore them with his resurrection power. What a privilege it is to be there when that happens!

TWO

HEALING AND THE
LOVE OF JESUS

In chapter 1, we noted that preaching, teaching, and healing were the primary activities of Jesus during his earthly ministry in Galilee (Matt. 4:23–24; 9:35). We also stressed that his ministry didn't come to a tragic end when he was crucified. In fact, it had only just begun. Following his resurrection and ascension, Jesus's ministry continues and expands throughout the world through his body, the church. Our involvement in the ministry of healing prayer is therefore a participation in his ongoing ministry, and particularly his healing ministry.

But what was it that moved Jesus to heal the sick and bind up the brokenhearted? What was the motivation behind his works of healing? Why did Jesus heal? That's the question we want to focus on in this chapter. In answering it, we begin by considering one of the greatest of all the healing miracles of Jesus—the raising of Lazarus as it's recounted in John 11.

At the very beginning of this story, Mary and Martha, Lazarus's sisters, send an urgent message to Jesus, letting him know that their brother desperately needs him: "Lord, the one you love is sick" (John 11:3). In a nutshell, that brief message answers a key question: Jesus's healing ministry flows out of his love. Because Mary and Martha understood this, they appealed to his love. THE MESSAGE captures it well: "Master, the one you love so very much is sick" (v. 3). Since Jesus loved their brother, they knew he would be concerned and would, no doubt, want to do something about Lazarus's illness.

Why then does Jesus heal? *Because he loves.* And as the Son of God, the love that moves him to heal is also a reflection of the love of the Father, because "he can do only what he sees his Father doing" (John 5:19). Ultimately, then, Jesus's healing ministry is rooted in the fellowship of the Trinity. Out of the overflow of the love of the Father, Son, and Holy Spirit, the triune God works to restore the brokenness of creation. Healing flows out of divine love and compassion. Certainly healing is an expression of God's power, but it's *more about God's love than about God's power.*

So, Jesus *healed* Lazarus because Jesus *loved* Lazarus. Three times in this story, his love for Lazarus is explicitly mentioned (John 11:3, 5, 36). We've already noted the first instance in the message the sisters sent to Jesus. Later in this chapter, we will discuss the second (v. 5). For now we will consider the last instance (v. 36) when, four days after Lazarus died, Jesus finally arrived on the scene.

At this point, Jesus was trying to comfort the two distraught, grieving sisters who couldn't understand why he didn't show up sooner. In the midst of all their tears and agony, the mourners who had come to grieve with Mary and Martha marveled at Jesus's intense emotional response and exclaimed, "See how he [Jesus] loved him!" (John 11:36).

The immediately preceding verse describes what they observed, which caused John to say, "Jesus wept." John 11:35 is the shortest verse in the Bible, as every Sunday school kid knows. Yet these two words say so much! "Jesus burst into tears," as the International Standard Version has it. He wept so openly, so intensely, and so vulnerably that those who saw him marveled and concluded, "Tears like that—he sure must have loved Lazarus."

My favorite series of books for children is the *Chronicles of Narnia* by C. S. Lewis. I say they are for children, but they are written for anyone who is truly young at heart. In one of them, *The Magician's Nephew*, there is a scene where Digory, a young boy, approaches Aslan the lion, who is the king of the land of Narnia where these stories take place. In case you didn't already know (although we're never explicitly told this), whenever you encounter Aslan, you are encountering another lion—Jesus, the great Lion of Judah.

Digory comes to Aslan because he has found out that in Narnia, when someone gets sick, they are given a piece of magic fruit to eat that causes them to get better. He wants to take a piece of the fruit back home with him because his mother is very ill and he wants her to get well. But Digory must get permission to do that, so he comes to make his request to the lion king.

Yet at first, when he asks, he gets no response at all. Aslan is silent. He seems indifferent. Digory is stunned— doesn't the lion care about his mother? Tears fill his eyes, and in desperation he comes closer and asks Aslan again. Here's how C. S. Lewis describes what Digory saw:

> Up till then he had been looking at the lion's great front feet and the huge claws on them; now in his despair, he looked up at its face. What he saw surprised him as much as anything in his whole life. For the tawny face was bent down near his and (wonder of wonders) great shining tears stood in the lion's eyes. They were such big bright tears compared with Digory's own that for a moment he felt as if the lion must really be sorrier about his mother than he was himself.[1]

From that moment on, Digory never again doubted the love of Aslan. "Whenever he remembered the shining tears in Aslan's eyes his heart became sure."[2]

Jesus wept at the grave of Lazarus. When he saw the anguish of Mary and Martha and the others gathered at the

tomb, big shining tears welled up in his eyes. *Jesus wept.*
And his healing of his friend Lazarus flowed out of his broken, weeping heart of love. Before Jesus heals our human hurts, he feels them!

THE COMPASSION OF JESUS

When we turn to the Synoptic Gospels (Matthew, Mark, and Luke), we also find the intimate connection between the love of Jesus and healing. These three gospel writers repeatedly emphasize how his healing ministry flows out of his compassion.

For example, Matthew 9:36, reads, "When he saw the crowds, *he had compassion on them*, because they were harassed and helpless, like sheep without a shepherd" (emphasis added). By the way, this verse immediately follows the one I've already referenced several times, describing Jesus's three major ministry activities in Galilee. Having told us *what* Jesus did (he preached, taught, and healed), Matthew also wants us to know *why* (because he had compassion).

Nine times in the Synoptic Gospels, Jesus is described as being moved with compassion. Four of these occurrences are directly linked with his healing ministry. Out of compassion, he healed those in a crowd who were sick (Matt. 14:14), cleansed a leper (Mark 1:41), raised the dead son of a grieving widow (Luke 7:13–14), and restored the sight of two blind men (Matt. 20:34).

In all nine cases, the gospel writers Matthew, Mark, and Luke, use *splanchnizomai,* the strongest possible Greek verb at their disposal, to convey the depth and intensity of Jesus's compassion.[3] No English translation can fully capture the meaning of this word. It was derived from the noun *splanchna,* which in classical Greek referred to one's inner organs, such as the heart, lungs, liver, and intestines. It was also used to refer to a mother's womb. Our English word *spleen* is derived from this word.

The Greeks believed that our inner parts were the seat of our deepest emotions—like anger, fear, and love. Based then, on its derivation, the verb *splanchnizomai* conveys no ordinary pity or compassion, but deep visceral emotion emerging from the core of one's being—like the gasp of a man overwhelmed with sorrow or the groaning of a woman in labor. To say that Jesus was "moved with compassion" meant that his gut was wrenched, his heart was torn open, and the most vulnerable part of his being was exposed.

No doubt Jesus's healing miracles serve more than one purpose. As we will see in chapter 5, they are unmistakable signs that the kingdom of God is at hand. They also reveal that Jesus is in fact the Messiah and the divine Son of God. We need then to recognize the various purposes of healing miracles. Yet though each is important, what moves Jesus to heal, first and foremost, are his love and compassion. His healing miracles are an expression of his love and the love of the Father and the Holy Spirit to those in great need.

Ken Blue sums it up well: "The gospel writers state that

Jesus healed people because he loved them. Very simply, he had compassion for them; he was on their side, he wanted to solve their problems." He adds, "God himself [in the person of Jesus] is distressed by our plight, and his emotional response is powerful. Mighty acts of rescue, healing and deliverance flow from his compassion."[4]

THE LOVE OF JESUS DETERMINES OUR PURPOSE

This vital connection between healing and the love of Jesus has many practical implications for the way we engage in healing ministry. That's why it's so important for us to grasp this. In the rest of this chapter, I will discuss four of them. Let's begin with how it shapes our understanding of the *purpose* of healing ministry.

It is easy in healing ministry, particularly in the case of physical healing, to get fixated on divine power and spectacle, to get overly excited about miracles, signs, and wonders. And it *is* exciting when we witness an instantaneous physical healing happening right before our eyes. When the deaf hear, the blind see, or the paralyzed walk, how can we *not* stand in awe and cheer and praise God. Given our proneness to discouragement and unbelief, we need to see miracles from time to time. As Raniero Cantalamessa suggests, God uses them "to break down and get rid of both dead ritualism and arid rationalism."[5] Such manifestations of divine power ignite our faith and deepen our conviction that God is real.

Healing ministry, however, is more about love than about power. The healing power of Jesus is an expression of his love—love that cares deeply about the immediate, felt needs of hurting, broken people. Healing power is necessary because Jesus's love is imminently practical and down-to-earth. In the face of sickness, pain, and suffering, it's not enough to send a Hallmark card!

But Jesus's healing power is always rooted in his love. It's the power *of love*. Love seeks the well-being of the other, is intent on deepening a relationship with the other, and wants to see the beloved flourish. Power for power's sake, power that seeks to manipulate and control, is a pagan notion—not a Christian understanding of power grounded in love.

Dan Wilt is a wise pastor who has spent several decades engaging in healing ministry in a church context that wholeheartedly embraces healing ministry and spiritual gifts. He has experienced firsthand what happens when healing ministry gets enamored with power, and he has learned how important it is to keep the focus on God's love:

I have at times seen a fixation on an experience of power and spectacle as the goal. When a limb is healed right there on the spot, it's exciting! When blindness is healed and a person sees for the first time in years, it's wonderful!

But the healing is not the point of what is happening in that moment. It never is. The love of God for the person is the most amazing thing happening in that moment. When someone's eyes light up with the love of God, expressed in quiet tears or loud rejoicing at what God has done, I'm pretty sure the angels in heaven are dancing—whether a "miracle" occurs or not!

I am so grateful for those who mentored me in praying for the sick and those in need. Those men and women would always remind me that the very least a person should leave with after a time of me praying for them is a deeper experience of the love of God. When a person feels that Jesus sees them, and knows them, it can trigger a deep inner healing to which even a physical healing can seem secondary. God's love brings an eternal miracle of union with the person. That is always the Father's goal.[6]

Over the years, as I have led numerous public healing services in local churches, my experience has been similar. Often in those services, as I've laid hands on and prayed for people, especially those with physical needs, I've watched them enveloped in Jesus's deep love and compassion for them. As a result, whether they experience physical healing or the healing they were hoping for, they slowly walk away in stunned amazement, with glad expressions on their faces, overcome with a deep sense of joy and peace that trumps everything else.

Seeing this happen right before my eyes has brought me great joy and satisfaction. Many times I've exuberantly walked away thinking, *This is so wonderful, I want to keep doing this for the rest of my life—even if no one I pray for is actually physically healed!*

Often when people come to us for healing prayer, they are primarily seeking a solution to a problem and are hoping we can help fix it or make it go away. Of course, Jesus cares about their problems; he weeps over them. But even more than solving their problems or bringing them comfort and relief, he wants them to know and experience his great love for them. He is longing for more intimate fellowship with them and is inviting them into a deeper relationship with himself.

Recognizing that this is Jesus's ultimate concern sheds light on what our primary concern in healing prayer should be: not solving problems but communicating Christ's love. Again, Dan Wilt spells it out well: "We won't get hung up on whether our prayers for them 'worked' or not. We will stay focused on God's love for the person as we pray. That focus will cause us to be sensitive in our praying, rather than distracted by a fix-it mentality, or overly dramatic trying to work up emotion."[7]

THE LOVE OF JESUS
SHAPES OUR PRACTICE

In addition to determining our purpose, understanding that healing is more about conveying love than demonstrating power will also shape our *practice* and have significant implications for the way we conduct healing ministry.

A former seminary student recently told me of her experience when she went to a church in her community to attend a healing service. She had never been to the church before and knew little about it, but she was weary and had been wounded in ministry. So when she learned they were having a healing service, she was eager to be there and was hoping to receive healing prayer.

Unfortunately, the way the prayer time was conducted made her very uncomfortable. After a time of worshipful singing and a brief message from the pastor, those who desired healing were invited to come forward to receive prayer. Then, as those who had responded stood there, they were smacked on the head and shoved backward as the prayer ministers declared, "Be healed in the name of Jesus." "When I saw what they were doing," she told me, "I stayed in my seat and did not go forward."

A pastor friend recounted a similar experience he had many years ago. He had recently become a Christ follower and was passionate about his faith, sincerely seeking more of Christ. When an invitation to receive prayer for healing was given in a worship service, he gladly went forward. "When they began to pray for me," he told me, "they literally 'karate chopped' me on both sides of my neck and then pushed me over. I was stunned and confused, wondering what in the world was going on."

These, of course, are extreme examples of what I would call abuses of power in healing ministry. Yet they are far too common and often give healing ministry a bad reputation.

They reflect what can happen when healing becomes too much about power.

To the Christians at Corinth who were overly enamored with spiritual power, the apostle Paul repeatedly stressed that they needed to "do everything in love" (1 Cor. 16:14; see also 8:1; 13:1–13). What he advised certainly applies to the way we conduct healing ministry.

We must always safeguard and preserve the dignity of people. We don't touch or lay our hands on people without their permission. We don't force people to do or say things if they are unwilling or uncomfortable. If they need to forgive someone, for example, we might say, "Are you willing to pray and forgive them for the wrong that they did to you?" If they tell us they are not, we respect their decision and don't try to force, manipulate, or shame them into doing so. We wait until the time comes when they are ready and willing.

Jesus has given us authority to heal in his name (Luke 9:1–2; Matt. 28:16–20), and there are occasions when we are led to pray authoritative prayers for healing. But remember that a bold, strong, authoritative prayer doesn't have to be loud, boisterous, dramatic, or overpowering. As I once heard a wise healing ministry veteran say, "Love is the muscle in the arm of authority." So everything should be conducted in a loving way.

This means that those of us who are involved in the ministry of healing prayer must continue to grow in our own capacity both to receive Christ's love and convey his love to others. Paul prayed that "being rooted and established in love" we would be able "to grasp how wide and long and high and deep is the love of Christ" (Eph. 3:17–18). That should be our prayer: "Lord deepen me and widen me in love."

Tilda Norberg, author of several profound, helpful books on healing, says it well: "Much of the emotional and spiritual preparation for doing this work has to do with being able to love more fully. . . . Loving means to invite God—daily, hourly—to love through us. Because our own love is incomplete and subject to distortion, we depend on God to fill us with the love we need to journey with another person. . . . Loving is not always easy. We must constantly work to rid ourselves of judgments, agendas, resentments, and fear."[8]

THE LOVE OF JESUS KEEPS US PATIENT

Understanding that Jesus's healing ministry flows out of his love not only determines the purpose of our healing ministry and shapes our practice; it also keeps us *patient* and steady when we are confronted with the mystery and complexities of healing.

In the Lazarus story discussed earlier, Jesus didn't initially heal Lazarus the way Mary and Martha wanted or expected. He showed up four days too late, four days after

Lazarus had died. And when he did arrive on the scene, both sisters—first Martha, then Mary—let Jesus know how frustrated and disappointed they were with him. "Lord," they complained, "if you had been here, [our] brother would not have died" (John 11:21, 32).

Like Mary and Martha, when we are engaged in healing prayer ministry with someone, we, too, can get confused and frustrated with what Jesus is up to. Why doesn't he step in and do something? Why doesn't he give us clearer guidance on how to pray? Why doesn't he answer our prayers? Often during the process, those seeking healing begin to doubt and despair. They wonder why Jesus doesn't seem to care.

Staying focused on Jesus's love steadies us and keeps us patient. Even though we can't trace his *hand*, we know we can still trust his *heart*. Interestingly, in the case of Lazarus, the reason why Jesus *didn't* come at once, like the sisters expected, was bound up with his love for them. As the text says, "Now Jesus loved Martha and her sister and Lazarus, so when he heard that Lazarus was sick, he stayed where he was two more days, and then he said to his disciples, 'Let us go back to Judea'" (John 11:5–7).

It was the love of Jesus, then, that caused him to show up four days too late. Oswald Chambers said, in reflecting on what Jesus did, sometimes "God's silences are his answers."[9] Yet when he did show up, that same love caused him to weep over the sisters' grief and cry out at the tomb, "Lazarus, come out!" (John 11:43). We see that his love can take many shapes and forms. It certainly isn't once-size-fits-all in its expression.

Knowing the compassionate, loving heart of Jesus helps keep us patient, steady, and on track. Regardless of what's happening, we can confidently declare, "Lord, we can't seem to trace your hand right now, and we're not sure how and when you are going to work in this situation. But Lord, we know we can trust your heart. We are sure of that. We know you weep over this situation. We know you love this person. Your compassion never fails. Regardless of how you choose to work in this situation, we know that nothing can separate us from your love."

When Digory "remembered the shining tears in Aslan's eyes, he became sure."[10] Keeping our eyes on the love of Jesus and the shining tears in his eyes keeps us patient and confident as we engage in healing prayer ministry. Regardless of what's happening or doesn't seem to be happening, we know we can count on that.

THE LOVE OF JESUS AND PERSISTENCE

We've talked about how rooting and grounding healing ministry in the love of Jesus determines our purpose, shapes our practice, and keeps us patient when the process is confusing and complicated. Let me close this chapter by stressing how it also undergirds our *persistence* in healing ministry.

As a local church pastor, seminary professor, and healing prayer minister, for the last fifty years I've been involved in all three major activities of the ministry of Jesus—preaching, teaching, and healing. But I must say that I've gotten into far more trouble and experienced more pushback over healing than over the other two combined!

Many Christians are critical and skeptical about healing ministry. And I can certainly understand why. Some who are drawn to it are overly enamored with the sensational and the miraculous. Others, in their zeal, go to dangerous, unhealthy extremes in their teaching and practice. Like Simon the magician (Acts 8:9–24), there will always be charlatans around who will try to take advantage of desperate people. As a result, healing ministry has developed a bad reputation, causing many pastors and leaders to shy away from it. To avoid its pitfalls and dangers, they prefer to avoid it altogether.

Often they look disparagingly on those who are called to it. "Why do you want to get involved in a ministry like that?" they will ask critically. "It's so complex, ambiguous, and controversial. And what about the people who don't get healed when you pray for them? Won't you end up disillusioning them?"

To be sure, these are all important and legitimate questions. In chapter 6 I address them as I discuss the mystery of healing. But when I have been interrogated about my involvement in healing ministry, after having acknowledged the person's valid concerns, here's what I usually say: "Let me be clear: I'm not involved in this because I'm enamored with healing. Nor am I the least bit interested in being known for having a healing ministry. But I am interested in being involved in the ministry of Jesus. I want to let my heart be broken by the things that break his heart, and to weep over the things that cause him to weep. I want to be drawn into his love and compassion. And then I want to follow him and join him in doing whatever he chooses to do as a result. That's why I'm involved in healing ministry."

In the first verse of what many consider his greatest hymn—"Love Divine, All Loves Excelling"—Charles Wesley summed it all up: "Jesus, Thou art all compassion; pure, unbounded love Thou art. Visit us with thy salvation; enter ev'ry trembling heart."[11]

This is what causes me to *persist* in healing ministry despite the concerns and criticisms of others. Through the *Holy Spirit*, I want to get connected to the love of *Jesus*, which, in turn, reflects the *Father's* heart of love and compassion. And then I want to be an open channel through which this Trinitarian love can enter the broken, trembling hearts of others. According to John Wesley, Charles's famous younger brother, such love divine, from which all healing flows, is "the sovereign remedy for all miseries."[12]

THREE

THE FIVE WAYS
JESUS HEALS

S he wasn't expecting to find what she did. In the introduction to her in-depth study *Healing in the History of Christianity*, Amanda Porterfield acknowledges, "When I embarked on this book, I did not anticipate the extent to which I would come to see Christianity as a religion of healing."[1] Carefully sifting through two thousand years of Christian history, she was struck by the wide variety of ways Christians have engaged in the ministry of healing. Through praying for supernatural healing, offering pastoral care, alleviating suffering with medicine, visiting the sick, caring for the dying, fostering healthy communities, building hospitals, training doctors and nurses, sending out medical missionaries, advocating health care access and reform, and encouraging practices that promote physical and mental health, Christians for two millennia—one way or another—have been involved in various forms of healing ministry.

As Amanda Porterfield discovered, healing is part and parcel of the Christian DNA. And partnering with Jesus in his ongoing healing ministry can take many shapes and forms. According to the New Testament, he is the one through whom all things were made (John 1:3; Col. 1:16; Heb. 1:2), all things hold together (Col. 1:17; Heb. 1:3), and all things are being made new (2 Cor. 5:17; Rev. 21:5). As Lord of both creation and new creation, he can heal in various ways.

So having established *why* Jesus heals—because he loves—I now want to focus on *how* Jesus heals by considering the five ways Jesus heals—what have sometimes been called "the five miracles of healing."[2] We can simply describe them as follows:

- Jesus heals directly and supernaturally—the miracle of the supernatural touch.
- Jesus heals through doctors and medicine—the miracle of modern medicine.
- Jesus heals through the human body's healing power—the miracle of nature.
- Jesus heals through bestowing grace in suffering—the miracle of sufficient grace.
- Jesus heals through victorious dying—the miracle of the victorious crossing.

As we engage in healing ministry it is imperative that we recognize and affirm all five of these ways Jesus heals. In this chapter, we'll briefly reflect on each of them, one at a time. And having done that, I will offer John Wesley as a model for us today of someone who rightly took them all into account.

JESUS HEALS DIRECTLY AND SUPERNATURALLY

As I emphasize particularly in chapter 5, Jesus's healing miracles demonstrate that the kingdom of God has arrived. In the person of Jesus the Messiah, what was expected to happen in the future at the very end of time when all things would be made new has broken into the present. Even now the lame walk, the deaf hear, the blind see, the dead are raised, and captives are set free! And when Jesus sent his apostles and disciples out preaching the gospel of the kingdom, he also gave them authority to heal in his name (Matt. 10:1–8; Luke 9:1–2). We see them continuing to exercise that authority after his resurrection and ascension in the book of Acts.

Unfortunately, down through the centuries Christians have often failed to exercise the authority Christ gave us in praying for direct supernatural healing for the sick. Sometimes they have even been discouraged by their leaders from doing so. For example, Martin Luther and

John Calvin took a dim view of miraculous divine healing. Reacting against excesses and superstitions associated with medieval Roman Catholic healing practices, these Protestant leaders argued that healing miracles had ceased after the first few Christian centuries. To be sure, during the time of the apostles, miracles and healings were needed to get the church launched. However, once the church was established and the New Testament was completed, miracles were no longer necessary. The preaching of the Word of God alone was sufficient for the spread of the gospel.

The influence of this teaching, known as *cessationism*, persists in many North American churches today. Fortunately, over the past 150 years there has been a growing involvement with supernatural healing among Christians. What began as a trickle with the Holiness healing revival of the late nineteenth century (1875–1900) became a widening stream in the Pentecostal, charismatic, and Third Wave movements (1900–2000), and has now become a flood with the rise of global Christianity in Africa, Asia, and Latin America (1985–2023). As a result, we have truly witnessed what the late Francis MacNutt called a "Healing Reawakening."[3]

In her introduction to *Global Pentecostal and Charismatic Healing*, Candy Gunther Brown sums up this reawakening like this: "Divine healing practices are an essential marker of Pentecostal and Charismatic Christianity as a

THE FIVE WAYS JESUS HEALS

global phenomenon. . . . In the Latin American, Asian, and African countries . . . as many as 80–90 percent of first-generation Christians attribute their conversions *primarily* to having received divine healing for themselves or a family member . . . and as Christians in the global South increasingly influence North American Christianity, divine healing will likely become even more prominent in the U.S. churches in the twenty-first century."[4]

No one has made the case for miracles as powerfully as New Testament scholar Craig Keener. In 2011 he published an exhaustive two-volume, 1,100-page work titled *Miracles: The Credibility of the New Testament Accounts*[5] and then ten years later followed it up with a shorter book called *Miracles Today: The Supernatural Work of God in the Modern World*,[6] in which he recounts the verified miraculous experiences of scores of people around the world. Never has there been a time in history when so many Christians are experiencing miraculous healings and taking authority to heal in Jesus's name.

Yes, the kingdom of God is at hand! Jesus continues to heal supernaturally through his body, the church. Granted, the majority of those we pray for will not be directly, supernaturally healed. As I stress in chapter 5, the kingdom of God is both *already* and *not yet*. Nevertheless, we should actively pray for miracles and expect supernatural inbreakings of the kingdom. Certainly this is one significant way Jesus heals today.

JESUS HEALS THROUGH DOCTORS AND MEDICINE

Yet Jesus also heals through doctors and medicine. This is why Christians have always held physicians and medical practice in high regard. According to Amanda Porterfield, rooted in their concern for healing and desire to alleviate human suffering, "Christians have constantly found themselves involved with medicine and concerned about the relationship between medical practice and religious faith."[7]

Generally, Christian beliefs and practices are rooted in the Old Testament. But in case you haven't noticed, doctors are rarely mentioned there. As Michael Brown observes in his meticulous study on healing in the Old Testament, there is "little evidence of widespread, specialized medical activity in ancient Israel."[8]

Yet it turns out there is good reason for this. Since the pagan priests were also the medical practitioners in the ancient world, looking to them for help was considered a violation of the first commandment, a form of idolatry, tantamount to consulting a pagan god and engaging in magic.

That's exactly what Asa, an Israelite king was criticized for doing. At the end of his life, when the disease in his feet became severe, we are told "he did not seek help from the LORD, but only from the physicians" (2 Chron. 16:12). Unfortunately, that verse has sometimes been used by well-meaning Christians as a proof text for not going to the doctor when they are sick but having faith in God alone for healing. Yet as Brown explains, "The fatal sin of Asa, king of Judah, was not primarily that of looking to doctors for help. Rather he was guilty of consulting pagan, or at least magical or idolatrous physicians in his time of extremity, rather than turning to the Lord."[9]

Fortunately, because of the influence of Hippocrates (c. 460–370 BCE) and others, the practice of medicine would develop in the Greco-Roman world as a distinct discipline of its own, separate from pagan religion and magical arts. As a result, Jews in the Hellenistic period took a much more positive view of doctors and medicine. Ben Sira, a Hellenistic Jewish scribe (second century BCE), expressed it like this:

> Give doctors the honor they deserve, for the Lord gave them their work to do. Their skill came from the Most High, and kings reward them for it. . . .
>
> The Lord created medicines from the earth, and a sensible person will not hesitate to use them. Didn't a tree once make bitter water fit to drink, so that the Lord's power might be known? He gave medical knowledge to human beings, so that we would praise him for the miracles he performs. . . .
>
> My child, when you get sick, don't ignore it. Pray to the Lord and he will make you well. . . . Then call the doctor—for the Lord created him—and keep him at your side; you need him. (Sirach 38:1–12 GNT)

The New Testament reflects this positive view of doctors and medicine as well. Luke, the Gentile author of over 25 percent of the New Testament, was a doctor. New Testament scholars have pointed out how often in his writings he used specific Greek medical terminology to describe illnesses and physical conditions. When he accompanied Paul on his missionary journeys, he served as his personal physician. Paul, in fact, called Luke "the beloved physician" (Col. 4:14 KJV).

Amanda Porterfield shows how this affirmative view of doctors and medicine has continued through two thousand years of Christian history. In *Healing in the History of Christianity*, she includes an entire chapter on "Christianity and the Global Development of Scientific Medicine,"[10] underscoring the important part nineteenth- and twentieth-century Christian missionaries played in this process. "They were the first to introduce scientific medicine in many parts of the world and their leadership as practitioners and proponents of scientific medicine played historic roles in making health care an important component of global development."[11] It was typical, wherever they went, for missionaries to build churches, schools, and *hospitals*.

Yes, Jesus heals supernaturally, but he also heals through doctors and medicine. Aware of it or not, they partner with him in his work of healing. So we should pray for our doctors, asking Jesus to guide and work through them both in diagnosing our illnesses and prescribing proper treatment and medication. Those of us in healing prayer ministry should work in tandem with doctors and mental health professionals. Therefore, we should encourage people to visit their doctors and be sure to heed their advice.

It is unfortunate when well-meaning Christians mistakenly set supernatural healing over against healing through doctors. Recently, a Christian leader told me about visiting an elderly woman who had suffered her whole life with problems in her feet. Not knowing this, as he was praying for her at the end of their visit, Jesus clearly said to him, "Take hold of her feet."

He was very hesitant and began to mentally argue with the Lord as he continued to pray. After resisting several times, he reluctantly obeyed. "When I placed my hands on her feet," he told me, "it was as if a jolt of electricity passed through my hands and her feet were completely and dramatically healed."

"You don't know this," she joyfully explained to my friend afterward, "but when I was a little girl, the Lord told me someday he would heal my feet. And today he has!"

This encounter led to a genuine friendship and partnership in the gospel that lasted until her death some years later. Sadly, however, she died virtually blind and unable to read her Bible or play the piano and organ (she was an accomplished musician)—all because she refused to get cataract surgery. "The Lord is my healer," she insisted. "I'm trusting in him alone to heal my eyes."

She was right—the Lord was her healer—but Jesus, who heals both directly and indirectly, often uses doctors and medicine to heal too. Allen Verhey summed it up well:

"Medicine is a good gift of God the creator, a gracious provision of God the provider, and a reflection and servant of God the redeemer. To condemn medicine because God is the healer would be like condemning government because God is the ruler, or condemning families because God is 'Abba.'"[12]

JESUS HEALS THROUGH THE HUMAN BODY'S HEALING POWER

Christ Jesus, the one in whom we "live and move and have our being" (Acts 17:28) and through whom we were "fearfully and wonderfully made" (Ps. 139:14), has designed us with bodies predisposed to healing. When we cut our skin, our blood coagulates and forms a scab, and the healing process begins. When our health is threatened by germs, bacteria, or viruses, phagocytes and leukocytes from our finely tuned immune system spring into action, producing antibodies that overcome the invaders, restore our health, and protect us from future attacks.

According to Jesus's design, our human bodies often heal themselves. The late Donald Demaray, my teacher and faculty colleague, told of spending a weekend in the home of a doctor who had been a highly respected general practitioner in his community for many years. "Sometimes, people just get well," he told Don. "I can't explain it. People with serious diseases may recover due to no medical treatment."[13]

Often in healing prayer ministry, I find myself working with people to address emotional, mental, and spiritual
issues that are preventing or diminishing the healing power
of their own bodies. Bitterness, unforgiveness, self-hatred,
contempt for our physical bodies, hypochondria—when
these issues are exposed and brought to Jesus, it's not unu-
sual for physical problems stemming from these to disappear
on their own.

In *A Doctor's Casebook in the Light of the Bible*, Paul
Tournier told of a doctor who for several months had been
unsuccessfully treating a woman who had severe anemia.[14]
Then, much to his surprise, her low white blood count
suddenly shot up to normal. "Tell me," he inquired, "has
anything out of the ordinary happened to you since we
last met?"

"Come to think of it, something has happened," she
answered. "I was finally able to forgive someone I've held a
nasty grudge against for a long time. And when I did, it was
as if I could begin saying 'Yes' to life again." Often, when we
remove spiritual and emotional barriers, then our "fearfully
and wonderfully made" bodies (Ps. 139:14) are set free to
do their healing work.

Furthermore, all the various ways we promote the health
of the human body must be taken into account. A proper
nutritional diet, regular exercise, sufficient rest and sleep,
recreation, laughter and play, community and social interac-
tion, solitude and retreat—all of these are vitally important
because they enable our bodies to keep us healthy and whole.

JESUS HEALS THROUGH
GRACE SUFFICIENT

Rather than removing the source of our suffering or pain, sometimes Jesus heals in a way we weren't expecting by imparting his grace and overcoming strength to us during our affliction. In his second letter to the Corinthians, Paul shared candidly about his own experience of such a healing by mentioning a "thorn in [the] flesh" (2 Cor. 12:7) with which he had to contend.[15] *Skolops*, the Greek word for "thorn," can mean either a stake that actually pegged a person to the ground or a splinter that was constantly irritating and defied extraction.

Because he didn't explicitly say what it was, there has been much conjecture about the exact nature of Paul's "thorn." Was it a particular person who relentlessly opposed Paul, persecution in general, a besetting sin or temptation, a speech impediment, or a physical infirmity such as epilepsy or an eye disorder? Bible scholars have put forward all of these as possibilities, but no one knows for sure.

Paul called his thorn "a messenger of Satan, to torment me" (2 Cor. 12:7). He viewed it as something evil that was intended to thwart God's purposes for him. So at first he vigorously and persistently prayed for its removal: "Three times I pleaded with the Lord to take it away from me" (12:8). His specific mention of praying three times reminds us of how Christ prayed three times in Gethsemane, "If it is possible, may this cup be taken from me" (Matt. 26:39).

However, Paul's thorn was not taken away. Instead, he clearly heard the Lord say, "My grace is sufficient for you, for my power is made perfect in weakness" (2 Cor. 12:9). Jesus's response to Paul's thorn was not to remove it, but to give Paul grace to endure patiently and joyfully, and to use Paul's resulting weakness to demonstrate divine power during it. For as Paul claimed, God's power is *perfected* in weakness.

No doubt God could have demonstrated his power by removing it. But by not removing it, God chose to do something even greater, to perfect his power through weakness. This transformed Paul's attitude toward his thorn. Instead of feeling defeated or causing him to wallow in self-pity, the weakness it produced gave him something to boast about. "I will boast all the more gladly about my weaknesses," he exclaimed, "so that Christ's power may rest on me" (2 Cor. 12:9). Instead of fueling frustration and dissatisfaction in Paul, his thorn-produced weakness caused him to experience contentment. "That is why, for Christ's sake, I delight in weaknesses. . . . For when I am weak, then I am strong" (2 Cor. 12:10).

We, too, may wonder why Jesus doesn't heal by removing some distressing "thorn" from our lives. Yet as Raniero Cantalamessa suggests, it may mean that, as with Paul, Jesus is "offering us a gift that is far more precious . . . even though it may be difficult for us to accept." In relation to some physical affliction, for example, Jesus may not take it away. But physical health, though precious, is only temporary and will one day pass away. By contrast, "to have borne suffering with patience is something good that will last for eternity."[16]

What a truly wonderful miracle of healing it is when we see people bearing suffering with patience through God's grace. I can think of a number of instances I have witnessed where the impact of one who has borne suffering with patience, yes, even with overflowing joy, has been greater in drawing others to Christ than if they had been instantly healed.

JESUS HEALS THROUGH VICTORIOUS DYING

According to the writer of Hebrews, through his death on the cross Jesus has destroyed "the power of him who holds the power of death—that is, the devil—and [freed] those who all their lives were held in slavery by their fear of death" (Heb. 2:14–15). Likewise, Paul triumphantly declared that since Christ has been raised from the dead, "death has been swallowed up in victory" (1 Cor. 15:54).

Yet make no mistake, Christians still must confront the dark reality of death with all its pain, sorrow, and agony. We grieve deeply when friends and loved ones die, and we grieve with those who grieve. But as Paul said, we grieve not "as others do who have no hope" (1 Thess. 4:13 NRSV). In the light of Christ's resurrection, we have been set free from our fear of death (Heb. 2:15). Its sting has been removed (1 Cor. 15:55–57) for it cannot separate us from the love of God in Christ (Rom. 8:38–39).

In fact, Paul came to view death as a doorway opening to a deeper, richer experience of God's love. He insisted that "for to me, to live is Christ and *to die is gain*" (Phil. 1:21, emphasis added). For to be "absent from the body" is to be "present with the Lord" (2 Cor. 5:8 KJV).

Death, tragic as it is, has been transformed by the risen Christ and has become for the Christian a means of healing. As Christian philosopher Peter Kreeft eloquently put it, "Christ has made Death into life's golden chariot, sent to fetch his Cinderella bride out of the cinders of this fireplace of a world, through a far midnight ride, to his very own castle and bedchamber, where Glory will beget glory upon us forever."[17]

I heard the wife of a pastor describe how she came to realize how Christ has transformed death. Her seventy-year-old mother had been in the hospital for over a week. But she was not responding to treatment and seemed to be getting worse. Each day she had been praying often and earnestly for her dear mother.

Then one night she woke up at 3 a.m. with another strong urge to pray. After about a half hour, suddenly her burden for her mother was lifted as she believed she heard the Lord Jesus distinctly say, "Your mother is healed." After that a deep peace engulfed her and she returned to sleep.

She awoke at 6 a.m. and called the hospital, expecting

to hear that her mother's condition had improved. Instead, the nurse in charge informed her that her mother had died in the early morning hours, around 3:30. "I was surprised and disappointed," she admitted. "Because I was so sure of what the Lord said in the night, along with the sense of peace I had, it wasn't what I was expecting. But then as I reflected on Jesus's words, I realized he *had* healed her. Now she was with the Lord—in his presence as never before."

For the Christian, Jesus has transformed death into a doorway of healing. Sometimes when we pray for someone, especially the elderly, we will be led to pray not for a dramatic miraculous form of healing, such as when Jesus raised Lazarus (John 11:1–44), but for victorious dying that will usher them into the very presence of Jesus and will demonstrate to others that Jesus has conquered death.

PARTICIPATING IN JESUS'S WIDE-RANGING HEALING MINISTRY

It is important that those of us who engage in healing ministry recognize, affirm, and take into account *all five* of the ways Jesus heals. Moreover, we shouldn't elevate one above the others or set them over against each other. Sometimes Jesus heals through more than one way at the same time. We might say to a person suffering with a physical illness, "You need to receive all the prayer for healing you can and get the best medical treatment you can."

In the past, Christians from different backgrounds and traditions have often failed to take all five ways Jesus heals into account. I was raised in the evangelical tradition, and we were strong on Jesus's healing through doctors and medicine. We also emphasized his sufficient grace for those who were suffering. Though we believed in the possibility of supernatural healing, in practice we seldom expected or prayed for Jesus to heal that way. Your experience may have been similar or distinctly different from mine. Maybe you grew up in the Pentecostal or charismatic tradition where you prayed regularly and often for supernatural healing but failed to properly emphasize other ways Jesus heals.

As we follow Jesus the Healer, we must recover his wide-ranging, holistic ministry of healing. It's time for his followers to recognize the vital importance of each of the five ways Jesus heals and to engage in a balanced, integrated, full-orbed practice of them all. I can't emphasize that enough.

Of course, given your calling, gifting, and expertise, Jesus may not have you focusing on all five. For example, you may be a pastor or a nurse, a medical doctor, an evangelist, a physical trainer, a nutritionist, a hospital chaplain, a professional counselor, a healing prayer minister, or a hospice worker. Your involvement in Christ's healing ministry may only focus on one or two of the five ways he heals. And that's the way it should be. All I ask is that you recognize and affirm all five ways Jesus heals. And you should encourage people to explore them all and seek out those who are gifted in each as needed. The point is, you can recognize and affirm the wide range of Christ's healing ministry even though in practice you engage primarily in one or two.

Understanding the five ways Jesus heals also shapes the way we pray for people. Sometimes well-meaning Christians pray, "Lord, *if it be your will*, heal so-and-so." Though I appreciate their concern to be humble and not presumptuous, I don't pray like this. Instead, I pray, "Lord, heal *according to your will*."

In light of the five ways Jesus heals, I am convinced he *always* wills to heal. The question is not *whether* Jesus wills to heal; the question is *how* does Jesus want to heal this person at this particular time? Through which of the five ways does Jesus will to heal? Does he want to use a combination of them?

Sometimes, as I am asking Jesus to lead me, I have clarity and confidence about this. But often when I pray, I really don't know. In that case, I begin praying humbly but confidently for direct supernatural healing. As we'll see in chapter 5, Jesus proclaimed that in his person and ministry, the future kingdom of God had arrived. Yet, although the kingdom was truly present when he was on earth in a physical body, it was also not yet fully present as it would be at the end of time. I begin with the *already* rather than the *not yet*, to stress that healing is for *today* and not only *someday*. So, I begin praying expectantly for a supernatural healing now. But if that doesn't happen, I will move on to pray in relation to one or more of the other ways Jesus heals that reflect the *not yet* of the kingdom. Regardless of which one I am praying for, I am always doing it within the framework of all five.

JOHN WESLEY AND THE FIVE WAYS JESUS HEALS

As we will see in the next chapter, John Wesley (1703–91) understood salvation not primarily in legal terms, as the forgiveness of sins, but as the restoration, recovery, and renewal of the image of God. Consequently, he had a deep and abiding interest in healing. Moreover, in his practice he was truly ahead of his time in emphasizing all five ways Jesus heals. I will spend the rest of this chapter briefly describing his involvement in each of them because he serves as a wonderful model for us.

Regarding supernatural healing, unlike many ecclesiastical leaders in his day, Wesley was not a cessationist who believed that healing miracles were restricted to the age of the apostles or the first three centuries of the church. He was convinced that miracles declined not because they were no longer necessary but because the hearts of believers eventually grew cold and hard. Having only a form of godliness, they lack boldness and power (cf. 2 Tim. 3:5).[18]

According to Wesley scholar Robert Webster, "Throughout his lifetime [Wesley] unabashedly embraced a belief in the supernatural and was convinced that an affirmation of the invisible world was an important component in the mission and ministry of Christianity in general and his Methodist societies in particular."[19] Belief and expectation of the supernatural, Webster maintains, was an essential strand in the original Methodist DNA. Scattered throughout his journal, as well as *Arminian Magazine*, which Wesley published for his followers, are specific accounts of supernatural healings among the early Methodists.

For example, in his journal entry for Thursday, October 7, 1790, he told of visiting with a Mrs. Jones, a devout Methodist who had suffered in pain for many years due to a collapsed uterus. Various doctors had treated her, but her condition only worsened. Finally, having been bedridden for two months, she cried out, "Lord, if thou wilt, thou canst make me whole! Be it according to thy will!" Immediately, the pain and the disorder ceased and she arose and dressed herself. In fact, from that hour, she had enjoyed perfect health. "I think our Lord never wrought a plainer miracle, even in the days of his flesh," Wesley concluded.[20]

Wesley believed in supernatural healing, but he also held doctors and medicine in high esteem. Because poor people in his day had little or no access to physicians, as a desperate expedient Wesley decided, "I will prepare, and give them physic [medicine] myself." He read widely in medical journals and consulted pharmacists, surgeons, and doctors in order to give them "the best advice I could and the best medicines I had."[21] The result was the establishment of a number of medical clinics among the Methodist societies and, most importantly, the publication of *Primitive Physic* for ordinary people. By far Wesley's bestselling book, it went through twenty-three editions during his lifetime, earning him $750,000 in royalties, most of which he gave away. Many of the recommended remedies and cures he included seem strange and even comical today, but in the eighteenth century they were the best treatments fledgling medical science had to offer.

Because he recognized the natural healing powers of the human body, Wesley practiced "holistic medicine" by regularly instructing his followers as to the importance of proper diet, regular exercise, and appropriate sleep and rest. Don't expect to receive much benefit from these remedies, he warned the readers of his *Primitive Physic*, if you disregard these crucial habits and practices. To the aristocratic Lady Maxwell, he advised, "Exercise, especially as the spring comes on will be of greater service to your health than a hundred medicines."[22]

Wesley also clearly understood the impact our thoughts and emotions have on our bodies. In fact, he criticized the doctors of his day for often failing to take this into account. "They prescribe drug upon drug, without knowing a jot of the matter concerning the root of the disorder. . . . Why then do not all physicians consider how far bodily disorders are caused or influenced by the mind?"[23] In most cases, "Till the passion [emotion] which caused the disease is calmed, medicine is applied in vain."[24]

You can find Wesley's emphasis on healing through

sufficient grace in affliction in published sermons such as "On Patience," and "Heaviness through Manifold Temptations." There is also an entire section labeled "For Believers Suffering," in the 1780 *Collection of Hymns for the Use of the People Called Methodist.*[25] Charles Wesley, who wrote most of these hymns, was convinced that suffering and growth in holiness were closely linked.

As a pastor and spiritual director to many, John Wesley often wrote letters of encouragement to Methodists who had told him about their suffering and affliction. To one such dear woman, Mrs. Woodhouse, he wrote, "Though sometimes it should be a grievous cross, yet bear your cross, and it will bear you: your labor shall not be in vain. Is not our Lord just now ready to bless you to increase your faith, and love, and patience? . . . Surely His grace is sufficient for you: sufficient to subdue all things to Himself."[26]

Healing through victorious dying is reflected in the many accounts of "happy deaths" Wesley included in his journal and in *Arminian Magazine.*[27] About a woman named Betty Fairbridge, he wrote, "But her bodily weakness increased: so much the more did her faith and love increase; till prayer was swallowed up in praise, and she went away with triumphant joy." John Bennets also died well: "A little before his death, he examined each of his children concerning their abiding in the faith. Being satisfied of this, he told them, 'Now I have no doubt that we shall meet again at the right of our Lord.' He then cheerfully committed his soul to him, and fell asleep."[28]

As a result, the early Methodists were known for dying well.[29] A physician who treated a number of them told Charles Wesley, "Most people die for fear of dying; but, I never met with such people as yours. They are none of them afraid of death, but [are] calm, and patient and resigned to the last."[30]

Much more could be said about Wesley regarding his involvement in each of the five ways Jesus heals. I strongly commend him to you as a model for healing ministry today. Of course, today we certainly have far more scientific knowledge in all five of these areas than Wesley did. But we can still learn from how he held these five together in an integrated, balanced way. In his emphasis on all five ways that Jesus heals, Wesley was ahead of his time and remains someone we should all seek to emulate.

FOUR

HEALING AND THE IMAGE OF GOD

M uch of what we believe about healing is rooted in our view of human nature. What does a flourishing, healthy, fulfilled human being look like? Why do humans need healing in the first place? What do they need to be healed from? And for what purpose? How we answer these questions stems from our understanding of human nature and the human person and shapes our practice of Christian healing.

Christians have always maintained that to understand human nature it is essential to go back to the beginning, to the first two chapters in the Christian story—creation and fall—as recounted in Genesis 1–3. So that's what we'll do in this chapter. In the last chapter we put a wide-angle lens on our camera to capture the breadth of the ways Jesus heals.

Now we will replace that wide-angle lens with a zoom lens to examine what the first two chapters of the Bible tell us about being created in the image of God (Gen. 1:26–27).

We must keep in mind what the New Testament writers emphasize—that Jesus himself is the perfect image (*eikon*) of God (2 Cor. 4:4; Col. 1:15), "the radiance of God's glory and the exact representation of his being" (Heb. 1:3). He embodies the image of God for us and is the perfect model of human personhood that God originally intended for us. In fact, according to the apostle Paul, God has "predestined [us] to be conformed to the image of his Son" (Rom. 8:29).

CREATED IN GOD'S IMAGE

Christians sometimes quibble about unimportant theological issues. But according to theologian Ray Anderson, the concept of the image of God is "not one of those issues. It is the foundational concept for understanding the biblical teaching concerning the nature and value of human personhood . . . [and] touches virtually every other tenet of Christian belief."[1]

According to Genesis 1–2, on the sixth day of creation God created human beings as the apex of creation. The biblical writer described it like this: "Then God said, 'Let us make humans in our image, according to our likeness; and let them have dominion over the fish of the sea, and over the birds of the air, and over the cattle, and over all the wild animals of the earth, and over every creeping thing that creeps upon the earth.' So God created humans in his image, in the image of God he created them; male and female he created them" (Gen. 1:26–27 NRSV).

Yet what exactly is the image of God? An "image," based on the etymology of the Hebrew word (*selem*), is a "representative likeness." Human beings therefore mirror or *reflect* God and *represent* God, like an ambassador from a foreign country represents their country. But exactly how do humans mirror or reflect God? Throughout two thousand years of Christian history, theologians and biblical scholars have proposed a variety of different answers to that question. I once took a semester-long course on the image of God and learned about them all, so let me save you the trouble of taking that class and sum up for you what I learned.

Throughout Christian history, there have been three major views concerning the image of God. The first, the *substantive* view, identifies the image with certain capacities or characteristics human beings possess. Those who adhere to this view most commonly identify the image with our capacity to reason; others with our capacity to make moral choices, or to know and worship God, or to enter loving relationships with others. Over the centuries, this way of understanding the image—as a particular human capacity—has been the dominant one.

The second, the *functional* view, identifies the image with something we were created to *do*. Human beings, according to the Genesis account, were given authority by

God to exercise dominion over the earth. Immediately after declaring, "Let us make humans in our image," the Lord God said, "and let them have dominion over the fish of the sea . . . the birds of the air . . . the cattle . . . the wild animals . . . and over every creeping thing that creeps upon the earth" (Gen. 1:26 NRSV). The next verse essentially repeats what has just been said: "So God created humans in his image . . . and God said to them, 'Be fruitful and multiply, and fill the earth and subdue it; and have dominion over . . . every living thing that moves upon the earth" (vv. 27–28 NRSV). In describing God's high regard for human beings, the writer of Psalm 8 echoed these verses in Genesis: "You made them rulers over the works of your hands; you put everything under their feet" (Ps. 8:6).

According to this view, as image bearers human beings are to exercise authority over creation. God has given us a "creation mandate" or "stewardship mandate" as it's sometimes called, to fill, subdue, and rule over the earth. We are expected to use our God-given abilities to understand and master creation.

The third major view of the image, known as the *relational* view, stresses that humans, like the triune God, are beings who exist in relationship. Those who hold this view stress that immediately after God declared, "Let us make humans in our image" (Gen. 1:26 NRSV), the verse says, "So God created humans in his image, in the image of God he created them; *male and female* he created them" (v. 27 NRSV, emphasis added).

According to this view, to be created in God's image is to exist as persons in relationship. Just as God exists as a community of persons—the Father, Son, and Holy Spirit—so we are fully human persons only in community. Created in God's image, human beings are unique in the created order in that we are capable of genuine relationships. In fact, according to Genesis 1–2 we exist in four relationships that are distinct but also closely interrelated.

First, Adam and Eve were created in relationship with God. God conversed with them (Gen. 2:16–17; 3:8–13) and had fellowship with them (3:8). They were capable of hearing God's voice and talking with God. Second, they were in relationship with each other (2:18–25). As partners, as husband and wife, Adam and Eve found joy and fulfillment in one another.

Third, they were in relationship with the natural order. Formed from the dust of the earth (Gen. 2:7), they were part of the material, physical world and were placed in the garden of Eden "to work it and take care of it" (v. 15).

Finally, humans exist in relationship with themselves in that they have the capacity for self-reflection and experience joy (Gen. 2:23). Initially Adam and Eve were self-confident in that they were "naked, and they felt no shame" (Gen. 2:25).

According to this relational view, being "created in God's image" means that human beings are constituted by these four relationships—with God (spiritual), with other humans (social), with the natural world (physical), and with themselves (psychological).

Substantive, functional, relational—these are the three major views of the image of God found in Christian history. And no doubt, a plausible case can be made for each. In addition, a growing number of theologians and biblical scholars today are advocating an inclusive view of the divine image that encompasses all three—capacities, functions, and relationships.

For example, Nonna Harrison sees the divine image as present "not simply in one or two of these aspects of human identity but in all of them. They are many facets of the splendid jewel that each human person can become."[2] Likewise, according to Cornelius Plantinga, the image of God "may plausibly be said to consist . . . in the whole set of these (and many more) likenesses. . . . The image will thus emerge as a rich, multi-faceted reality, comprising acts, relations, capacities, virtues, dispositions, and even emotions."[3] Finally, Anthony Hoekema states that by the image of God "we mean the entire endowment of gifts and capacities that enable man to function as he should in his various relationships and callings."[4]

In case you're wondering, the inclusive view is the one I advocate as well. And I especially appreciate the way Hoekema expresses it since I like to view the various *capacities* (rational, volitional, spiritual, etc.) and *functions* (working, serving, loving, ruling) associated with the image as necessary, not as ends in themselves, but as means to an end so we can live out God's intended purpose or goal for us in the four *relationships*—with God, others, the world, and ourselves.⁵ Figure 4.1 below depicts the image of God in Genesis 1–2 in light of these four relationships as they were originally intended.

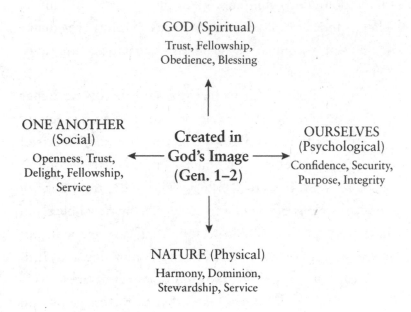

GOD (Spiritual)
Trust, Fellowship,
Obedience, Blessing

ONE ANOTHER (Social)
Openness, Trust,
Delight, Fellowship,
Service

Created in
God's Image
(Gen. 1–2)

OURSELVES (Psychological)
Confidence, Security,
Purpose, Integrity

NATURE (Physical)
Harmony, Dominion,
Stewardship, Service

THE RESTORATION OF THE IMAGE OF GOD

Unfortunately, because of Adam and Eve's tragic turning away from God and fall into sin (Gen. 3), human beings have lost their ability to fulfill God's intended purpose in the four relationships. As a result of sin, our capacities and functions have become severely damaged and marred. All four relationships still exist, but they have also been profoundly affected. The image of God has become a broken image.

In light of Genesis 3, figure 4.2 depicts what has happened to the four relationships as a result of the fall:

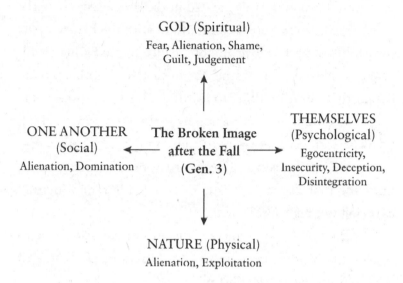

GOD (Spiritual)
Fear, Alienation, Shame,
Guilt, Judgement

ONE ANOTHER The Broken Image THEMSELVES
(Social) ← after the Fall → (Psychological)
Alienation, Domination (Gen. 3) Egocentricity,
Insecurity, Deception,
Disintegration

NATURE (Physical)
Alienation, Exploitation

Consequently, we have been banished from the garden and can never go back (Gen. 3:23–24). Like Humpty Dumpty, we have "had a great fall." There is nothing we can do to solve the problem. No matter how hard we try, despite all our striving or pulling ourselves up by our own bootstraps—we can't fix ourselves. "All the king's horses and all the king's men can't put [us] back together again." We need outside help. Happy thoughts and bootstraps won't do; we need rescuing.

Of course, that is why God himself has come in the person of his Son Jesus, who is the Word made flesh (John 1:14–18) and the second Adam (Rom. 5:12–19). Moreover, as I said earlier and as the New Testament explicitly states (2 Cor. 4:4; Col. 1:15; Heb. 1:3), he himself is the *eikon*, the image of God, the exact representation who perfectly embodies God's intention for humanity as created in the divine image.

As the beloved Son in communion with the Father, Jesus lived a life of perfect love and obedience to the Father's will. As he was loved by his Father, he in turn loved others to the extent that he was willing to lay down his life for them. He exercised dominion over nature by stilling a storm, walking on water, and feeding a multitude with a few loaves and fishes. He also possessed a proper relationship with himself, knowing that he was his Father's beloved Son and joyfully carrying out his Father's will.

As the Son of Man and second Adam, he also came to restore the broken image in us. As Jesus said, he "came to seek and to save the lost" (Luke 19:10). He came to restore what was lost and distorted because of the fall, so that those who believe in him might be transformed and conformed to his image (Rom. 8:29; 2 Cor. 3:18).

According to John Wesley, this is what salvation in Christ is primarily and fundamentally about. It is not merely "deliverance from hell, or going to heaven, but a present deliverance from sin, a restoration of the soul to its primitive health . . . the renewal of our souls after the image of God in righteousness and true holiness, in justice, mercy, and truth."[6] This, Wesley insisted, is "the great end of religion . . . to renew our hearts in the image of God, to repair that total loss of righteousness and true holiness which we sustained by the sin of our first parent."[7]

THE IMAGE OF GOD AND HEALING

Understanding what it means to be created in God's image is central to what Christians believe about human beings and about salvation. It is also crucial and foundational for healing ministry. Frank Bateman Stanger, who wrote and taught extensively on healing during the years when he was president of Asbury Theological Seminary (1962–82), summed it up well: "The church's ministry of healing rests fundamentally upon the nature of men and women, as created by God in his own image. . . . Jesus healed persons rather than merely curing diseases. . . . The healed person is restored and set once again within [their] true destiny."[8]

As the healing ministry of Jesus continues in the world today through his body, the church, Jesus continues to heal persons by both restoring the broken image and conforming them to his own image. For those of us engaged in healing ministry, let's consider what this means as we seek to follow Jesus the Healer and the "exact representation" of the divine image (Heb. 1:3).

When a person comes to us for healing prayer, often they will talk to us about a specific problem in a particular area of their life. Sometimes it's a physical problem ("I have severe arthritis in my hands"). Or it may be an emotional problem ("Recently, I have felt so overwhelmed with fear and anxiety"). Or a spiritual problem ("God seems so far removed and distant from me right now").

What they describe is the "presenting problem" and often the reason they've come to us for help. And certainly, when we pray for them, we should honor their request and pray for their perceived healing need. It's not uncommon as we converse with them or pray for them to begin by focusing on that point of need.

Yet often what they perceive to be their need may be too narrow. It may only have to do with one or two of the four relationships (spiritual, social, psychological, physical) which constitute the image of God. As we listen to and pray for them, we need to be thinking in broader terms. We need to be seeking to discern how their "presenting problem" might be affecting each of the four relationships that constitute the divine image in them.

Granted, it may not be affecting each relationship to the same degree and may be affecting some more than others. But because healing is about the restoration of the image of God, we need to be attentive to all four relationships.

When a person requests healing prayer for a physical need in their life—"I have painful arthritis in my hands," for example—in addition to asking them questions about their physical condition ("How long have you suffered with this? When did it start? What does your doctor think is causing it? Are you taking medicine to alleviate it? Does it get worse at certain times?"), we should also be wondering about the various relationships in their life.

How has this has affected their relationship with God? Do they believe God has let this happen because he's upset with them about something? Do they feel disappointed and let down by God for allowing this condition? Are they angry at God or having a hard time trusting God because of it?

How has this affected their relationship with others? Has this condition removed them from friends and community? Has it led to social isolation? What do they think others are saying about them? Do they feel embarrassed and not want to be seen in public? Do they think others are being critical and looking down on them?

And what about their relationship with themselves? Do they feel ashamed for having this condition? Do they think they've done something to deserve this condition? Are they angry with themselves and blaming themselves for it?

As we listen to them, we should be praying and asking the Holy Spirit to reveal what might be going on in each of these areas. We may also want to probe gently with a few questions concerning these various other relationships so that we can include them as we pray.

Time and again, I have been amazed when I have taken these steps. For example, when people come forward for prayer in a healing service I'm conducting in a local church, I will simply ask, "What do you want Jesus to do for you?" Often they will describe some physical need they have. But because of time constraints, we can't really engage in conversation where I might ask the kinds of questions I've just described. So I will pray, "Come, Lord Jesus; come, Holy Spirit"; and after pausing for five or ten seconds, I will begin praying for their physical need.

But then as we continue (often I am working with a prayer partner), though I may be tentative and unsure, I may pray along these lines: "Lord, if this physical condition has affected their relationship with you, if it has caused them to become disappointed or angry with you, or made it difficult for them to trust you, would you come right now and assure them of your love for them. Would you communicate to them how you are feeling toward them right now."

I can't tell you how often, as I've prayed like this, I've watched as tears fill the person's eyes. Jesus comes and conveys his deep love and compassion for them. When we've finished praying, their tears have turned to joy. Whether they experience physical healing or not, there has been a healing and renewal in their relationship with God. For they have experienced the love and compassion and reassurance of Jesus in whose presence, in the words of the psalmist, there is "fulness of joy" (Ps. 16:11 KJV).

Understanding that every person we pray for is a person created in God's image significantly affects the way we pray for healing. All four relationships need to be taken into account, and often we discover how interrelated and intertwined they are. Truly, each affects the others.

Sometimes forgiving someone who has wronged us (social healing) or forgiving ourselves for a past failure or regret (psychological healing) results in the healing of our bodies (physical). I know of a number of cases where a person let go of a nasty grudge they had held toward someone for a number of years and, without even asking for it, also received healing for a physical problem they had. When they forgave, the physical problem just seemed to disappear on its own.

HOW JESUS HEALED

The more I've studied the healing miracles of Jesus recorded in the Gospels, the more I've come to realize that this was, in fact, the way Jesus went about healing. In his insightful book *Healing in the New Testament*, New Testament scholar John Pilch draws on insights from the emerging field of medical anthropology to shed light on the healing ministry of Jesus. Medical anthropology—in case you've never heard of it—studies the way sickness is viewed in various cultures, both past and present. Experts in the field often distinguish between "disease" and "illness." "Disease," according to Pilch, is a narrower term that "derives from a biomedical perspective that sees abnormalities in the structure and/or function of organ systems. . . . Disease affects individuals, and only individuals are treated."[9] Illness, on the other hand, is a broader term that "derives from a socio-cultural perspective" and takes into account how sick people perceive themselves and how they are viewed by their communities. Illness therefore "inevitably affects others: the significant other, the family, the neighborhood, the village."[10]

Most Americans and Europeans, in light of modern medical science, tend to view sickness primarily in biomedical terms as "disease." However, the rest of the world, what we might call the majority world, views it primarily in personal and social terms as "illness." First-century Jews viewed it as illness as well, as did Jesus. That's what Frank Stanger was getting at when he said that "Jesus healed persons rather than merely curing diseases." His concern was for the whole person and all four of the relational dimensions of the image we've talked about.

Think, for example, of the woman who had suffered with a hemorrhage, most likely involving vaginal, menstrual bleeding, for twelve years (Mark 5:25–34). She had spent all she had on doctors "yet instead of getting better she grew worse" (v. 26).

That was bad enough. Yet in addition to her long-term physical problem, consider that according to Jewish law as spelled out in Leviticus 15:25–27, her physical ailment made her ritually unclean. According to New Testament scholar William Barclay, that meant "she could never attend a synagogue service; no one could lie on the same bed as she; no one could even sit on the same chair. She was cut off from all religious and social life . . . shut out from the worship of God and from the society of her friends, and even her family."[11]

Yet despite all that, when the woman heard about Jesus the Healer, faith rose within her. "If I just touch his clothes," she thought to herself, "*I will be healed*" (Mark 5:28, emphasis added). But how could she make contact with him? If she touched him, he would become unclean and so would anyone in the crowd who was touched. She was too embarrassed and afraid to go up to Jesus and tell him her predicament.

In her faith and desperation, the woman devised a plan. Like all religious Jews, as prescribed in Numbers 15:37–41, Jesus wore tassels on the corners of his robe. *If I could just touch one of them*, she thought to herself, *no one, not even Jesus, will notice. And I will be healed.* So that's what she did. And when she did, "immediately her bleeding stopped and she felt in her body that she was freed from her suffering" (Mark 5:29). What a miracle that was! After twelve years she was finally healed. And knowing that she had received the physical healing she so desperately longed for, I suspect that all she wanted to do was quietly slip away unnoticed.

Yet Jesus was intent on healing her whole person, not merely curing her disease. He knew that "power had gone out from him" (Mark 5:30), but he wanted to do more than heal the woman's body. So he stopped and insisted on finding out who in the crowd had touched him. The woman was no doubt ashamed and embarrassed; the last thing in the world she wanted was to be exposed like that. Finally, however, she came forward, "fell at his feet and, trembling with fear, told him the whole truth" (v. 33).

At that point, the woman was expecting to be severely reprimanded by Jesus and the crowd, but the very first word Jesus spoke to her changed everything: "Daughter." He didn't call her "woman," but "daughter"—an intensely personal term of endearment, a term that conferred dignity and belonging on her, that implied family and community. "Daughter, your faith has healed you. Go in peace and be freed from your suffering" (Mark 5:34).

Jesus commended the woman for her faith. He blessed her with *shalom*—peace with God, with herself, and with others. And he bestowed on her freedom and liberty. Put simply, all four dimensions of the broken divine image—spiritual, social, physical, and psychological—were restored.

Then and now Jesus seeks to heal the whole person. And he invites us to join him in a healing ministry like that.

FIVE

JESUS, HEALING, AND THE KINGDOM OF GOD

The kingdom of God was *the* central theme in the preaching of Jesus. As he traveled throughout Galilee, he proclaimed, "The time has come. . . . The kingdom of God has come near. Repent and believe the good news!" (Mark 1:15). The kingdom of God was also the central theme in his teaching in his Sermon on the Mount (Matt. 5–7) and his parables.

In this chapter, we want to consider the close relationship between the kingdom of God and healing—the other major activity, along with preaching and teaching, in the ministry of Jesus (Matt. 4:23; 9:35). And we want to reflect on the implications that relationship has for us as we join and follow Jesus in his ongoing ministry of healing.

HEALING AND THE ARRIVAL
OF THE KINGDOM

When Jesus announced the arrival of the kingdom, Jewish hopes and expectations of a coming Messiah, as foretold by Old Testament prophets, were running high. The Messiah, it was commonly believed, would soundly defeat God's enemies—and especially Israel's enemies—and bring an end to the present evil age of sin, suffering, sickness, and death. He would usher in the kingdom of God and the age to come. The Holy Spirit would be poured out. A new creation would dawn, and the dead would be raised. At last God would sovereignly, righteously, and peaceably rule over his people and the whole world. His original plan for creation would be restored.

So when Jesus came declaring, "The age to come is here; the kingdom of God is at hand," it was truly a big deal. He was claiming that the day the prophets had spoken of and that the people had been waiting for had arrived. Signs of the presence and activity of the kingdom were springing up for all to see. God's reign was so near it couldn't be ignored. What was happening demanded a response: "Repent and believe the good news."

Those signs were present in the *words* of Jesus—his preaching and teaching of the kingdom. And they were also present in his *deeds*—his mighty works, his miracles. And of course, this is exactly where healing comes in.

I've referred to Matthew's summary statement of the

threefold ministry of Jesus (Matt. 9:35) several times before. Earlier in his gospel, there is a similar but expanded statement describing what happened when Jesus first arrived on the scene:

> Jesus went throughout Galilee, teaching in their synagogues, proclaiming the good news of the kingdom, and healing every disease and sickness among the people. News about him spread all over Syria, and people brought to him all who were ill with various diseases, those suffering severe pain, the demon-possessed, those having seizures, and the paralyzed; and he healed them. Large crowds from Galilee, the Decapolis, Jerusalem, Judea and the region across the Jordan followed him. (4:23–25)

Notice how Matthew underscored the profound, immediate impact of Jesus's healing ministry. His healing miracles were *prima facie* evidence of the presence of the kingdom, signifying that the time was fulfilled and the kingdom of God was at hand. In fact, according to theologian Jürgen Moltmann, after the proclamation of the gospel, "the healing of the sick is Jesus's most important testimony to the dawning of the Kingdom of God."[1]

Healing also includes the expulsion of demons. In the passage just quoted, people brought their sick *and* their possessed to Jesus, and he healed both. This means God was now acting through the words and deeds of Jesus and was launching a frontal attack on the kingdom of Satan. Jesus had entered the strong man's house (Satan's kingdom) and bound him (Mark 3:27) so that men and women could be delivered from his power. Healing, and especially the expulsion of demons, is unmistakable evidence of this, and it signals the inbreaking of the kingdom of God. As biblical scholar George Eldon Ladd emphasized, "Jesus's power over demons was the disclosure that the powers of The Age to Come have invaded the present evil Age. It was the proof that the Kingdom of God, which belongs to the age of the future when Christ comes in glory, has already penetrated this Age."[2]

Some Jewish religious leaders attributed the undeniable power behind Jesus's exorcisms to Satan himself. Jesus countered, "If Satan drives out Satan, he is divided against himself. How then can his kingdom stand?" (Matt. 12:26). His power, he insisted, came from another source and signified a different kingdom: "But if it is by the Spirit of God that I drive out demons, then the kingdom of God has come upon you" (v. 28).

Jesus's ministry of healing—the healing of the sick and the expulsion of demons—is inextricably bound up with the kingdom of God. He proclaimed the kingdom through his words (preaching and teaching), and he enacted the kingdom through his deeds (healing).

This healing ministry also authenticated Jesus himself as the Messiah and King who ushered in the kingdom. When the imprisoned John the Baptist had doubts and wanted to know, "Are you the one who is to come, or should we expect someone else?" (Matt. 11:3), Jesus didn't give John a direct answer. He pointed, instead, to his healing ministry foretold by the prophet Isaiah (Isa. 35) as convincing evidence of who he was: "Go back and report to John what you hear and see: The blind receive sight, the lame walk, those who have leprosy are cured, the deaf hear, the dead are raised, and the good news is preached to the poor" (Matt. 11:4–5).

Jesus's healing ministry thus signaled the arrival of the messianic King and, in turn, the inauguration of the age to come, the kingdom of God. Healing, Messiah, kingdom of God—the three are inseparable. The nature and purpose of healing is therefore bound up with the nature and purpose of the kingdom ushered in by Jesus, the Messiah.

Understanding this is crucial for those of us engaged in healing ministry. It tells us that healing ministry doesn't operate as an end in itself or as a law unto itself. It must always be placed in its proper context—the kingdom of God. To rightly understand healing, we must rightly understand the kingdom.

THE MYSTERY OF THE KINGDOM

Yet rightly understanding the kingdom is not as simple as we might think. It certainly wasn't for the earliest disciples. Jesus did his best to help them understand, but even in his very last conversation with them, just before he ascended into heaven, they were still quite confused about the kingdom (Acts 1:6–7).

Like most first-century Jews, they believed that at the very end of time, God, through his Messiah, would bring a dramatic end to the present evil age (characterized by sin, suffering, sickness, and death). That end would also mark the beginning of the age to come, the kingdom of God characterized by righteousness, wholeness, resurrection of the dead, and the outpouring of the promised Spirit.

However, what Jesus did and what he taught messed with their timeline. What they expected to happen all at once at the climactic end, in the distant future, was beginning to happen in the here and now, in the immediate present. His healings and exorcisms were irrefutable evidence that the kingdom they believed would be ushered in at the very end of time had in fact *already come*. So was this the end? They were confused because Jesus also taught that the fullness of the kingdom was *yet to come*. He instructed his disciples to pray, "Your kingdom come, your will be done, on earth as it is in heaven" (Matt. 6:10). Likewise, in many of his parables, Jesus stressed that though the kingdom was *truly* present now, it was not *fully* present and would be consummated in the future. Like a tiny mustard seed, it had germinated and was growing. But it certainly wasn't the full-blown fruit-bearing tree it was destined to become. Like yeast, it was working in the loaf, but the dough still had a lot of rising to do (Matt. 13:31–33).

So, the Messiah King had come, and the kingdom had definitely broken in. The blind could see and the lame walk. Signs of new creation were present as never before. Yet all the while, the old creation was still very much present. Suffering, sickness, evil, and death—the evidence of Satan's kingdom—were still around. Wheat was springing up, but the weeds that an enemy had planted were also growing (Matt. 13:24–30). Not everyone was being healed (Mark 6:1–6; John 5:1–9), and those who were healed still eventually died.

So Jesus exhorted his disciples to watch and pray, to wait and work for the King's return, when he would come again in final glory to consummate the kingdom (Matt. 25). At that time, Satan, who had already been defeated, would be destroyed once and for all. Suffering, sin, and death would be no more. God would come and dwell among his people forever.

The kingdom and reign of God was both *already* here and *not yet* here. This was the mystery of the kingdom, and Jesus said that not everyone had eyes to see or perceive this mystery, the *dual nature* of the kingdom. That's why he taught in parables, so that it would remain a secret and a mystery to some, yet would be divinely revealed to others (Matt. 13:11–17).

Even Jesus's disciples didn't truly comprehend this most of the time. Like many first-century Jews, their kingdom perspective was myopic, nationalistic, and self-serving (Mark 10:35–45). They had heard Jesus's kingdom preaching and teaching. They had seen his kingdom healing miracles. They had confessed that he was, in fact, the Messiah, the one who had ushered in the kingdom (Mark 8:27–30). But they were still far too bound to a conventional Jewish way of thinking.

It was the resurrection of Jesus from the dead (Easter) and the pouring out of the Spirit (Pentecost) that finally altered their perspective. They were now confident that the kingdom reign of God and the future age to come and all the things they associated with it—resurrection from the dead, the fullness of the Spirit, the new creation—had in fact come and were already present. Yet they were also sure that because of the continuing presence of Satan, evil, suffering, and death, the kingdom was still yet to come and hadn't fully arrived. It was truly present, but only partially present, not fully. The kingdom would be finally and fully consummated when the King returned.

New Testament scholar Gordon Fee nicely summarized what they came to believe and how it shaped the way they lived:

> In place of the totally future, still-to-come end-time expectation of their Jewish roots, with its hope of a coming Messiah accompanied by the resurrection of the dead, the early believers recognized that the future had already been set in motion. The resurrection of Christ marked the beginning of the End, the turning of the ages.
>
> However, the End had only begun, they still awaited the final event, the (now second) coming of their Messiah Jesus, at which they too would experience the resurrection/transformation of the body. They lived "between the times"; *already* the future had begun, *not yet* had it been completely fulfilled. This already/not yet perspective, in

which they believed themselves already to be living in the time of End, even though it was yet to be consummated . . . determine[d] everything about them—how they lived, how they thought, and how they understood their own place in the present world, which was now understood to be on its way out.[3]

The earliest followers of Jesus lived in what Fee called "the radical middle"—between the beginning of the end and the consummation of the end—insisting that the future is both here (already) and not fully here (not yet). That's why the apostle Paul earnestly prayed for and regularly expected to see in-breakings and miraculous demonstrations of God's healing power, but he also stressed that such power was often manifested in weakness (2 Cor. 12:1–10). Kingdom power was "sometimes attested by signs and wonders and at other times by joy in great affliction."[4]

KINGDOM EXPECTANCY IN HEALING

This New Testament "radical middle" kingdom perspective is foundational for our understanding of healing. Let's consider its practical implications for healing ministry.

First of all, knowing that the kingdom of God is "here" undergirds our faith and increases our expectancy in Jesus's power and ability to heal *now*. In Luke's account (4:16–21),

Jesus began his public ministry in the synagogue in his hometown, Nazareth, when he opened the scroll and read from the prophet Isaiah. It is significant that after he had read the familiar passage ("The Spirit of the Lord is upon me . . ."), his own very first word recorded by Luke was "today." "*Today*, this scripture is fulfilled in your hearing" (Luke 4:21, emphasis added). Jesus was declaring that the time is now. The kingdom, the time of God's reign, when God's promises will be fulfilled, is *today*.

In healing ministry, because the kingdom of God has come in the person and ministry of Jesus, it is therefore always today.

Some Christians insist that healing is only for *yesterday* or *someday* but not for *today*. They don't deny that healing played a vital part in the ministry of Jesus and the apostles. At the beginning, it was necessary to get the church up and running. However, they insist that's not the case anymore since the church has been established. Healing, then, was for *yesterday*. Granted, it happened in the past, but it was for then—not now.

It is also for the future, for *someday* when Jesus returns. Then, as the Scripture says, "He will wipe every tear from their eyes. There will be no more death or mourning or crying or pain, for the old order of things has passed away" (Rev. 21:4). Yes, that will happen someday, but not now, in the present order of things. For now, we can look to Jesus for comfort and strength to endure suffering, but *not* for healing.

86

Given the growing body of evidence from church history that attests to the contrary[5] and, above all, given the huge role that healing has played in the in the growth of global Christianity in the last fifty years,[6] there are fewer and fewer who still doctrinally adhere to this position. Cessationists, as they are called, believe that, by and large, healing miracles ceased after the time of Jesus and the apostles.[7] Even if they would not strictly adhere to this position, many Christians today, especially in Europe and North America, function as *practical* cessationists. They doctrinally affirm the possibility of divine healing but never expect or believe it will happen.

In sharp contrast, for those of us shaped by a New Testament already/not yet view of the kingdom and seeking to live in the "radical middle," our first word in approaching healing ministry is *today*, not *yesterday* or *someday*. Though we understand the kingdom is both *already* (has come) and *not yet* (is coming), our starting point should be the *already* rather than the *not yet*. This means that we confidently declare the breakthrough of the kingdom. We boldly announce the age to come, the future age that has invaded this present age in the person and work of Jesus the Messiah, in his resurrection from the dead and the Pentecostal outpouring of the Holy Spirit. Yes, the kingdom of God has broken through. And it continues to break through every now and then, mysteriously and unpredictably no doubt, but surely and certainly, nonetheless.

When Jesus sent out his twelve disciples, he gave them these specific instructions: "As you go, proclaim this message:

'The kingdom of heaven has come near.' Heal the sick, raise the dead, cleanse those who have leprosy, drive out demons. Freely you have received; freely give" (Matt. 10:7–8). Later he sent out seventy-two others, instructing them that when they entered a town they were to "heal the sick who are there and tell them, 'The kingdom of God has come near to you'" (Luke 10:9).

Jesus commands his followers to do the same today—to proclaim the good news that the kingdom of God is near and to heal the sick. So we do what he says. We may be uncertain about how Jesus will work, unsure of ourselves, and concerned about disappointing others if nothing seems to happen. But with "fear and trembling" and deep humility, we boldly pray for healing because we want to be obedient to his commands. Ultimately, that's what compels us. Ken Blue is right: "The final reason for taking up the ministry of healing is simply out of obedience to Jesus Christ."[8] Moreover, to deny the possibility of healing today is to deny that what Jesus said about the presence of the kingdom now is true.

When we pray for healing, we certainly should not be presumptuous. But because we believe what Jesus says is true—the kingdom *is* here—we should pray boldly and confidently for healing, expecting it by faith and expecting it now. Derek Morphew says it well: "Every time you pray for the sick, you should be full of expectation. The veil has been rent. Anything is possible at any moment, including the freedom of the captives, the healing of the sick and the raising of the dead."[9]

THE MYSTERY OF THE KINGDOM AND HEALING

At the same time, however, we must humbly and frankly acknowledge that often those we pray for aren't healed the way we hoped or expected. Others are only healed partially. Still others, not at all. Even those who are miraculously and wondrously healed will eventually grow old and die. Yes, the kingdom is already, but it is also not yet. We must emphasize this as well. As Ladd explained, "In the [final] eschatological kingdom, all . . . will be saved from sickness and death in the immortal life of the resurrection. In the present working of the Kingdom, this saving power reached only a few. Not all the sick and crippled were saved, nor were all the dead raised. . . . The saving power of the Kingdom was not yet universally operative."[10]

This leads us to a second important implication that kingdom theology has for the ministry of healing: understanding that the kingdom is not yet fully come enables us to come to terms with the ambiguities and limitations associated with healing ministry.

A variety of human factors play a significant role in healing. Desperation (Mark 10:46–52), prayer (Mark 9:28–29; Luke 11:9–13; James 5:17–18), faith (Mark 5:34, 6:5–6; James 5:15), confession (James 5:16), obedience (Luke 17:11–14), gifting (1 Cor. 12:28; James 5:14)—these are a few mentioned in the New Testament. And they need to be taken into account. But it is always a mistake to reduce healing to a simplistic if-then formula based on any of them. It is a mistake to insist, for example, that *if only so-and-so had more faith . . . if only we had prayed and fasted more . . . if only someone more gifted had prayed . . . then that person would have been healed.*

Later we will examine the role faith plays in healing since there has been much misunderstanding and confusion about that. But the point we need to understand here is this: anytime we try to dismiss or deny the *not yet* dimension of the kingdom by making a human factor *ultimate* in healing, we will get into trouble.

Of course, human factors are significant; those who are experienced in healing ministry recognize how crucial they are. But because the kingdom of God is our context for healing, the already/not yet nature of the kingdom must always remain the ultimate consideration that informs our approach to ministry. Whenever someone is healed, that healing bears witness that the kingdom of God is already here. And whenever someone is not healed, the lack of healing bears witness that the kingdom of God is not yet here. What does and does not happen is rooted, first and foremost, in the *already/not yet* nature of the kingdom.

Whenever we pray for the sick, we should pray *boldly*, but we should also pray *humbly*. As Derek Morphew also wisely advises, "You should 'hang loose' in the mystery. When nothing happens do not be 'fazed' at all. After all, this is the 'not yet' dimension in which we live. Delayed answers to prayer, and things that are not yet here, are all part of the kingdom."[11]

Make no mistake—this is not always easy to do. "Hanging loose in the mystery," praying expectantly yet humbly, living in "the radical middle," avoiding the extremes of both presumption and unbelief, will often feel uncomfortable and unsettling. We will be tempted to resolve the already/not yet tension and remove the ambiguity and mystery of the kingdom.

Often others will encourage us to do that. "What you are saying is too complicated," they will complain. "Can't you make it simpler?" No, we can't. The kingdom of God cannot be reduced to a sound bite. Until the King returns, it will remain both—already and not yet. We must resist the urge to give in to their wishes, choosing instead to embrace the uncomfortable place of biblical tension rather than moving to a logical extreme that might appear to make more sense to others.

KINGDOM KEYS ARE HEALING KEYS

As I draw this chapter to a close, I want to briefly mention an additional implication a correct understanding of the kingdom of God has for healing ministry. Because the kingdom is the context for healing, what Jesus taught about the kingdom—specifically its nature and values as set forth in the Sermon on the Mount (Matt. 5–7) and kingdom parables—is essential for healing ministry as well.

The conditions that create a context for healing in people's lives are the same conditions that create a context for the inauguration and growth of the kingdom. Consider, for example, the familiar words of the Lord's Prayer, "Thy kingdom come, thy will be done, on earth as it is in heaven." Jesus was telling us that the presence of the kingdom increases and expands whenever and wherever God reigns and God's will is done.

In his *Letters on the Healing Ministry*, Albert Day (1884–1973) insightfully drew out the implication of this truth for our understanding and practice of healing:

> God acts in healing where God reigns. God does not reign where God's will is flouted. . . . Only where God truly reigns, where God's will is accepted, where the obedience and cooperation of people give God a free hand in their lives can God give them health in the place of disease, truth in the place of error, holiness in the place of vileness, and beauty for ashes. The prime condition for healing is therefore to enter the kingdom, to let God reign, to give God a free hand in one's life.[12]

Often those we pray for fail to receive healing because they refuse to accept and obey Jesus's kingdom principles. For example, when Peter asked Jesus how many times we should forgive someone who persists in sinning against us, Jesus said, "I do not say to you, up to seven times, but up to seventy-seven times" (Matt. 18:22 NASB). He went on to explain what this meant by telling a kingdom parable about an unforgiving servant (vv. 23–35).

Anyone who has been significantly involved in healing ministry will tell you how important a person's willingness to forgive others is to experiencing healing.[13] I once heard Charles Kraft say, "Unforgiveness keeps more people from receiving healing from God than anything else in the world." Understanding the kingdom context for healing reveals why.

Or consider the kingdom values Jesus set forth at the beginning of the Sermon on the Mount in the Beatitudes (Matt. 5:1–12). He said that those who would be blessed were the poor in spirit, those who mourn, the meek, those who hunger and thirst for righteousness, the merciful, the pure in heart, the peacemakers, and those who are persecuted because of their righteousness. All these keys to receiving the blessings of the kingdom are also keys to receiving healing blessings as well.

We can sum it up this way: the conditions for healing are in accordance with the conditions for our entrance, continuance, and growth in the kingdom. It's as simple as that.

SIX

EMBRACING
THE MYSTERY
OF HEALING

W hen I was in the eighth grade, my English teacher made our class memorize "Flower in the Crannied Wall," a six-line poem by the famous nineteenth-century Victorian poet Alfred Lord Tennyson:

Flower in the crannied wall,
I pluck you out of the crannies,
I hold you here, root and all, in my hand,
Little flower—but if I could understand
What you are, root and all, and all in all,
I should know what God and man is.[1]

I must confess, when I recited it, I had no clue what the poem meant. I wasn't even sure what a "crannied wall" was. Thankfully, it was only six lines and easy to memorize! But that poem has stuck with me down through the years. In fact, it's the only thing I can remember learning in that English class! And as time has passed, I've gained an appreciation for what Tennyson was trying to tell us.

We can hold a little flower in our hands. We can carefully observe and analyze it as an experienced botanist would. Yet even with a tiny, insignificant flower, we find ourselves in the presence of mystery. What is its essence? Where did it come from? Why is it like this? Who can say? There is so much here we don't know and can't wrap our minds around. And if that's the case even with a little flower, isn't that true about everything?

In all of life, we are confronted with an element of mystery, far more than we can know or fully comprehend. And as Christians who affirm the doctrine of the Trinity, we shouldn't be surprised. Our foundational belief that God is three in one and one in three tells us this as well. Although it's not an irrational or illogical belief, the Trinity transcends human reason. Our minds are incapable of fully grasping it. The catechism of the Catholic Church sums it up well: "The Trinity is the central mystery of the Christian faith and life. It is the source of all other mysteries of the Christian faith, the light that enlightens them."[2]

More than any other Christian doctrine, the Trinity sets before us the mystery of God and points to an element of mystery in every aspect of our faith. Our highest reasoning powers and most profound logical categories will never penetrate or comprehend, explain or contain, resolve or remove the mystery of God. Our finest words about God are but feeble, faltering attempts to express what can never fully or adequately be conveyed in any human language. God cannot be captured or imprisoned in any of our categories, and he repeatedly breaks out of our carefully constructed boxes.

At the same time, we must be clear that the mystery of the Trinity does not mean we know nothing definitive about God since "it's all a mystery anyway." In current English, a mystery is something obscure, dark, secret, or puzzling, like a murder mystery. If something is "mysterious," it's inexplicable, incomprehensible, and enigmatic. However, the Greek word used by the New Testament writers had a distinctively different meaning. Instead of an impenetrable, locked secret, it is an open secret, one that has been revealed.

The Trinity, like all the mysteries of the Christian faith, is a truth beyond human derivation or discovery. We only understand it because God has taken the initiative and revealed it to us. Because God "has spoken to us by his Son" (Heb. 1:2), Christians believe we have been given definitive knowledge of God. And so we confidently proclaim that God as Father, Son, and Holy Spirit is three in one and one in three.

Our definitive knowledge of God, however, is not exhaustive. As we *apprehend* God's triune self-revelation, we also acknowledge and gladly confess that we do not fully *comprehend* God. We are grateful that God has revealed himself to us, but we also recognize that the greater whole eludes our grasp.

HEALING MINISTRY AND MYSTERY

Because creation bears the marks of God's Trinitarian imprint, at every turn we find ourselves in the presence of mystery. Yet no area of Christian ministry forces us to grapple with it as much and as often as healing ministry. Anyone who has been significantly involved in this ministry will tell you, "Healing ministry is messy." And that's one of the major reasons many Christians avoid it.

It's messy because, again and again, it confronts us with mystery. As Ken Blue explains, "Despite the fact that God wills to heal the sick, not all the sick are healed. This ambiguity forces us to realize that we are dealing with a mystery: we are interacting with a sovereign and free God; we are confronting sin, demonic beings, and a host of complex psychological, physical and spiritual factors."[3]

When we earnestly pray for supernatural physical healing, sometimes those we pray for are not healed. At other times, they are healed of one thing but not another. I think of my pastor friend who was miraculously healed when his church leaders anointed him and earnestly prayed for severely ruptured discs in his back. But he has also been a diabetic for years and is careful to take insulin every day.

Sometimes Jesus heals when a person isn't even asking to be healed. A Christian leader from Australia told me about a Muslim man in Indonesia who wandered into a large outdoor evangelistic meeting where he was preaching. The man was just a curious bystander, but suddenly he was healed from debilitating chronic arthritis in his right shoulder and could raise his hand above his head for the first time in years.

Sometimes one person gets healed and another doesn't. A pastor from India was visiting in South Africa, and while he was there he prayed for the complete healing of a child who was HIV positive. This was not something he usually did, he told me, but because he felt strongly prompted by the Holy Spirit, he went ahead, and miraculously the child was healed. However, a few days later, at the request of a desperate mother, when he prayed for her HIV positive child, the child still died several days later.

I'll never forget an evening several decades ago when I was confronted with the mystery of healing at a seminary faculty prayer meeting. We were rejoicing because a sixty-year-old faculty colleague was sitting in our midst, praising God for his recent miraculous healing. Several weeks before, he had been at death's door because of the various complications following his open-heart surgery. I had been present at the healing service in the critical care unit when a dozen of us gathered around him and desperately and boldly prayed for his healing. From that point on, his condition began to improve dramatically.

Four weeks later, he was discharged from the hospital, and the doctors agreed it was a miracle. As his cardiologist said, "That meeting, when that group gathered around you and prayed—no doubt, that was the turning point." Now, a week after he had come home, he was sitting in our midst, a living witness to the supernatural healing power of Christ. And we all rejoiced and praised the Lord with him.

Yet at that same prayer meeting, we also listened as another professor requested prayer for the family of a bright, promising, twenty-five-year-old Asian seminary student who had been killed a few days before in a tragic car accident. The professor, who knew him quite well, had attended his funeral service that day and had spent time with the young man's heartbroken, grieving parents. What a senseless tragedy it was. He was a deeply committed Christian and had sacrificed a lucrative career to come to seminary. He had such a promising ministry ahead of him. Why had this happened? Couldn't God have protected him?

As I sat there, having listened intently to both professors—one rejoicing, the other grieving—I was struck by the stark, utter contradiction. In one case, God had acted so clearly and powerfully; in the other, God seemed absent and uninvolved. There was no way I could explain or make sense of it or resolve the tension between the two realities.

That evening, as we lifted our praise and our petitions to the Lord, though I couldn't logically resolve the contradiction, strangely, the contradiction was resolved within me. Somehow, in the midst of our prayer and worship, I found myself at peace with all my questions. *I don't know why it turned out this way. It really doesn't make sense,* I thought to myself. *But it's okay, Lord. I don't pretend to fathom your ways, but I trust in your character, in your wisdom and goodness.*

Over the years, as I've engaged in healing prayer ministry with seminary students, particularly in relation to emotional and spiritual issues in their lives, again and again I've found myself in the presence of mystery. For example, there is the mystery of suffering and evil. "How could God allow such an awful thing to happen to me?" I have often been asked. And I humbly confess that I don't really have a satisfactory answer.

Then there is the mystery of the way healing unfolds in a person's life. Sometimes Christ's healing power manifests in dramatic, miraculous ways, resulting in major breakthroughs. At other times, however, healing comes through a difficult, drawn out, deliberate process where every three steps forward are followed by two steps backward. On some occasions, I find myself praying boldly and authoritatively; yet on others I can only encourage someone to hold on in the darkness where God seems absent.

Finally, there is the mystery of God's strength being perfected in weakness. That which brought such evil into someone's life may be transformed into an instrument for good. What was once a cause of brokenness becomes a means of conveying Christ's fullness. The very place of someone's humiliation and shame has become their place of spiritual power and authority. In wonder and gratitude, I can only exclaim, "Lord, what an amazing thing you have done!"

BECOMING COMFORTABLE WITH MYSTERY

Mark it down: as you engage in healing ministry, expect to find yourself in the presence of mystery. You won't be able to avoid it, so don't try. Learn to become comfortable with mystery. This may not always be easy to do. Those you counsel and pray with may find living with mystery uncomfortable. When you refuse to "make it go away," you will be moving against the stream of their hopes and expectations. So here I'll offer three suggestions.

First, allow those occasions when you are confronted with the mystery of healing to cultivate and deepen humility in you. Think of it this way: when we don't have adequate answers, we feel weak, powerless, inadequate, and out of control. But although that's uncomfortable, it can deepen and enrich us spiritually because it strikes a blow at the root of our pride and self-sufficiency. Bumping up against the limits of our knowledge and understanding invites us to humble ourselves and stand in awe. In the presence of mystery, we find ourselves crying out, like the ancient Israelite king Jehoshaphat, "We do not know what to do, but our eyes are on you" (2 Chron. 20:12).

Second, recognize the way the paradoxical nature of truth is reflected in Christian healing. As I indicated earlier, the belief that an element of mystery pervades all things is rooted in the Christian understanding of the Trinity. God is one being in three persons and is never one without being three or three without being one. To speak the truth about God, we must firmly insist that both are true. We cannot assert one to the neglect of the other.

The Trinity presents us with two things—Three and One—which seem contradictory and incompatible. How can both equally be true? Yet they are. In order, then, to speak the truth about God, to express it rightly, we must use the language of paradox. Moreover, the Trinity is only the first of many paradoxes we encounter in the Christian faith (for example, Christ is fully human and fully divine; our salvation is the result of both divine sovereignty and human freedom).

Earlier, when we described the relationship between healing and the kingdom of God, we encountered paradox too. Jesus spoke about "the secret [or mystery] of the kingdom of God" (Mark 4:11) because the presence of the kingdom is both here (present) and near (future), both *already* and *not yet*. And we insisted that both dimensions be taken into account. In healing ministry, as we must cling to both and live in the "radical middle," we will often find ourselves in the presence of mystery.

There will always be those who are uncomfortable with paradox and will try to resolve the tension, the seeming contradiction of the *already/not yet*. They will elevate one side of the paradox to the neglect of the other, over-emphasizing the *already* at the expense of the *not yet* or the *not yet* at the expense of the *already*.

This seems logical and simple, so it will appeal to many. Yet although it appears plainer, it proves less truthful. The half-truth that is overemphasized to the neglect of the other ends up being a whole lie. For that's what error most often is: not the total absence of truth, but truth separated from its balancing counterpart. It is attractive because going to a logical extreme can be more comfortable than living in the paradox of biblical tension.

This leads to my third suggestion: resist the temptation to oversimplify healing. We live in an age that wants to evade mystery by reducing the complexity of things to a for-mula, a technology, a program, a quick fix, or a sound bite. Sadly, the landscape of Christian healing ministry is strewn with many tragic examples of this.

I'll never forget the tearful sharing of a forty-year-old man in a Sunday school class I was leading. When he was thirteen years old, his beloved elderly grandfather became critically ill. For days this young man prayed earnestly that God would heal his grandfather. He often visited him in the hospital. Eventually, however, his grandfather died, and he was heartbroken with grief. Unfortunately, his pastor made him feel even worse. "If you only had more faith," he said emphatically, "God would have healed your grandfather."

"In my mind, I know it's not true," he told our class, "but

103

ever since that time, I've felt like I was responsible for my grandfather's death, and I still sometimes feel guilty about it."

What deadly fruit his pastor's simplistic understanding of the place of faith in healing had borne in this man's life. As I stress later in this chapter, the relationship between faith and healing is paradoxical—it's both simple and complex.

My concern here is simply to urge you to resist the temptation to oversimplify healing. The late Francis MacNutt, who for decades was such a wise and gifted leader in healing ministry, said, "Just to know that healing is a mystery—that it's complicated and not all that simple—should free us from any need to give simplistic answers to people who wonder why they are not totally healed. To know how complex healing is helps us to rely more upon God's light, to seek real discernment, and to let go of simplified solutions."[4]

In the remainder of this chapter, I discuss two widespread teachings about healing that fall into the "simplified solutions" category. Both apply especially to supernatural *physical* healing. Those who adhere to them are often passionately involved in healing ministry and strongly believe in Christ's power to miraculously heal our bodies. Many have personally experienced physical healing themselves and have prayed for others who have also been healed.

However, in their passion for healing and zeal in encouraging others to look to Jesus for physical healing, they have fallen into error in their teaching, logical extremes that have led to tragic consequences in people's lives. In both instances, they oversimplify the paradoxical *already/not yet* nature of the kingdom of God, emphasizing the *already* at the expense of the *not yet*. The first concerns the relationship between the atonement of Christ and healing; the second revolves around the role of faith in healing. Let's consider them both, one at a time.

THE ATONEMENT AND PHYSICAL HEALING[5]

Surely he hath borne our griefs, and carried our sorrows: yet we did esteem him stricken, smitten of God, and afflicted.

But he was wounded for our transgressions, he was bruised for our iniquities: the chastisement of our peace was upon him; and with his stripes we are healed. (Isa. 53:4–5 KJV)

For two thousand years, Christians have believed that these words of the prophet Isaiah about the Suffering Servant who was to come best explain what Jesus was doing on the cross. He died on account of our sins. The apostle Peter, echoing Isaiah, declared, "'He himself bore *our sins*' in his body on the cross" (1 Peter 2:24, emphasis added). Similarly, Paul summed up the consensus of apostolic teaching: "Christ died *for our sins* according to the Scriptures" (1 Cor. 15:3, emphasis added).

Yet in his gospel, in quoting from Isaiah 53, Matthew

maintained that the prophet's words "He took up our infirmities and bore our diseases" were specifically fulfilled in Jesus's healing of the sick (Matt. 8:17). According to theologian Jürgen Moltmann, Matthew was inferring that Christ's healing power is "not to be found in his supreme power over sickness and disease. His power to heal is *the power of his suffering*. He heals by 'carrying' our sicknesses. 'Through his wounds we are healed' (Isa. 53.5). His passion and his self-surrender on Golgotha are the secret of his healings of the sick."[6]

Matthew's interpretation has therefore led some to conclude that on the cross Jesus bore our sicknesses and bodily diseases *in the same manner that he bore our sins*. Consequently, just as forgiveness of sins is guaranteed for us when we repent and believe (Acts 2:38), so, too, is healing for our physical illnesses when we pray in faith. Divine healing has therefore been secured for us "in the atonement" in the same way as divine forgiveness of sin.

Moreover, if that is true, it stands to reason that if you are *not* healed when you pray for physical healing, it's not because Jesus doesn't will it—he has made provision for it through his death on the cross just as he has made provision for forgiveness. The problem, then, if you don't receive healing, must be on your end. It may have to do with ignorance, unconfessed sin, failure to ask, lack of faith, persistence in prayer, or some other issue. But if you properly address and deal with those things, you will be healed. It's as simple as that.

Or is it? Consider all that was accomplished for our

salvation through Christ's atoning life, death, and resurrection. Along with the forgiveness of sins, the gift of the Holy Spirit, the resurrection of the body, life everlasting, and new creation, we would certainly include physical healing as well. All these "benefits of his passion," as an old Communion liturgy called them, are indeed rooted in his atonement. So it is certainly true to say that "healing is in the atonement."

But does that mean that these benefits of the atonement are all available to us *now* and in the *same way*? Based on the teaching of the whole New Testament, the clear answer is no. Some benefits we experience fully in the present, others only partially, and still others only in the future consummation of the kingdom.

It's better to speak of healing *through* the atonement than healing *in* the atonement. By doing so, we recognize that all healing is rooted in the atoning death of Christ, but we also avoid the implication that we are guaranteed physical healing in this life. Sam Storms says it well: "The question is not *whether* our bodies are healed because of the atonement of Christ but *when*. . . . It's a serious mistake to think every blessing Christ secured through his redemptive suffering will be ours now *in its consummate form*. All such blessings shall indeed be ours. But let us not expect— far less demand—that we now experience the fulness of blessings God clearly reserved for heaven in the age to come (Rev. 7:15–17; 21:3–4)."[7]

As Jesus repeatedly stressed, the kingdom of God is both

already and not yet. So are its blessings and benefits. Some, such as the forgiveness of sins, are *already*, while others, such as the redemption of our bodies, are *not yet*. Physical healing happens to fall somewhere in between—in the radical middle. Sometimes it's *already*, sometimes *not yet*, and sometimes a combination of the two. No wonder healing ministry is messy! So we have to live in the *already/not yet* tension and embrace the mystery.

THE ROLE OF FAITH IN HEALING[8]

Based on the gospel accounts of Jesus's healing ministry, faith plays a vital role in healing. Jesus looked for those who had faith (Mark 9:23, 28). In several instances, he directly attributed someone's healing to their faith (Mark 5:34; 10:52). Jesus commended those who demonstrated faith (Matt. 8:10; 9:22; 15:28) and rebuked others for their lack of faith (Luke 9:41). The unbelief he encountered in his hometown of Nazareth even limited what Jesus was able to do (Mark 6:5–6).

Those deeply involved in healing ministry today also recognize the critical link between faith and healing. Randy Clark, who has been significantly engaged in healing ministry for the past thirty years and has conducted healing crusades all over the world, expressed it like this: "I say it time after time—when more faith is present, more happens. The more faith that is present in a person the more likely he or she will receive healing. The more faith that is being expressed in an atmosphere, the more likely it will be that waves of healing will break out among that specific group of people. Faith is important."[9]

Yet does this mean that a direct cause-and-effect relationship exists between faith and healing? Absolutely not. This misguided "faith formula" teaching, as it's sometimes called, is a simplified solution that has led to disillusionment, heartache, confusion, and guilt in the lives of many. It is therefore a grave mistake to tell someone seeking healing, "If you only have faith, you can be certain you will be healed."

I appreciate the way Randy Clark, who rightly emphasizes the importance of expectant faith in healing, wisely steers clear of this teaching. "Jesus Himself worked with people at different faith levels," he observes. When we recognize this, it "immediately dispels the myth that 'you won't get healed if you don't have enough faith.'"[10]

For example, there were those like the woman with the issue of blood (Mark 5:25–34) and the blind man Bartimaeus (Mark 10:46–52), who had what Clark describes as "great faith" and "reckless faith." However, there were also those like the man with leprosy (Mark 1:40–45) and the father of the demonized son (Mark 9:17–29) who only had "some faith" and "very weak faith."[11] So Jesus heals people who have different levels of faith. In the cases of those who have only a weak or minimal expression of faith, Clark notes, "it is amazing how powerful is the simple act of coming to Jesus."[12]

In his in-depth study of Jesus's healing miracles, New Testament scholar Keith Warrington arrives at a similar conclusion. Jesus welcomed and healed those who doubted yet wanted to believe, like the father of the demonized boy who cried, "I do believe, help me overcome my unbelief!" (Mark 9:24). All the fitness and faith necessary was to feel their need and to come to Jesus. Warrington sums it up like this: "The faith that brought forth a response from Jesus is the readiness simply to go to him for help."[13]

Sometimes in faith formula teaching, the account of Jesus's rejection in his hometown of Nazareth where his healing power was limited "because of their unbelief" (Mark 6:1–6) has been used to prove that "if you only had more faith, you would be healed." In this case, however, as Warrington rightly maintains, their unbelief was not a case of weak faith or doubt. Jesus could work with that. In Nazareth, rather, their unbelief was rooted in a stubborn refusal to believe in Jesus, in a deliberate determination to reject him.

What, then, is the faith necessary for healing? Often people have been given the impression that it has to do with possessing a certain mental state or psychological certainty. In other words, "You must believe—*beyond a shadow of a doubt*—that Jesus will heal you. So rid your mind of all doubt."

Unfortunately, defining faith in those terms—as a state of mind—puts too much focus on us and what we must do to be healed. It is a burden too heavy for us to bear. By contrast, understanding faith simply as the readiness to go to Jesus for help puts the focus where it rightly belongs—on the person of Jesus. That's where our focus needs to be—on *him*, not on *us*. Not on how much faith *we have*, but on who *he is*, what he has done and promises to do.

And I can't think of a better way to end this chapter. As we navigate the profound mystery of healing, it is faith in the person of Jesus and our trust in his goodness and wisdom—not in an oversimplified formula or our own certainty—that holds us steady and keeps us moving forward. As Ken Blue has put it, "Faith to heal the sick is not bravado—it is the freedom to believe and act based on who Jesus Christ is. Our faith in the fight to heal is expressed in our acting, despite our doubts, on who we see Jesus to be."[14]

SEVEN

BY HIS WOUNDS
WE ARE HEALED

How could God have allowed something so awful and destructive to happen to me?" she exclaimed. "I was just an innocent little girl. My father and the other men who raped me were engaged in such horrendous evil. Where was God when that happened? How could he stand by and do nothing?"

She was a woman in her forties whose long-repressed memories of incest and abuse were slowly coming to the surface. A skilled counselor was carefully helping her navigate the process. A psychiatrist had prescribed antidepressants to help her manage feelings, which at times were chaotic and overwhelming. We would meet in my office every few weeks for times of healing prayer. And one day, about a week after an especially dark, painful layer of memories had come to light, she poured out her feelings of anger toward God about the evil and unjust suffering that had been inflicted upon her.

As you engage in the ministry of healing, you may never come face-to-face with the problem of suffering and evil as directly as I did that day. Yet sooner or later, as you walk with people, particularly into dark places of emotional pain and trauma, you will certainly be confronted with it. It is important, then, for you to reflect on this problem and work toward developing a theology of suffering. What follows in this chapter is intended to help you do that.

For some this problem of theodicy, as it's called, is primarily *philosophical and intellectual*. Simply stated: How can God, who is good and all-powerful, allow so much suffering—particularly unjust suffering—in the world? Is a god who lets the innocent suffer and permits senseless death worthy to be called God at all?

In Fyodor Dostoevsky's great nineteenth-century novel *The Brothers Karamazov*, the child of a poor Russian serf is playing one day and accidentally hits one of his master's prize hunting dogs with a stone. When the master finds out about it, he is enraged. He has the boy seized and turns his vicious dogs loose, forcing the boy's mother to watch as they tear her son to pieces.

When Ivan, one of the main characters in the story, hears about what the master has done, he shakes his head in disbelief. After a long reflection on how a good and righteous God could allow such a thing to happen, he concludes, "It's not God that I cannot accept. . . . I accept God, understand that, but I cannot accept the world that He has made."[1] Like Ivan and many who reject the Christian faith today, the magnitude of unjust suffering in the world has become the cornerstone in their wall of unbelief. But it's not only unbelievers who wrestle with this problem. Many believers do too, even though they may be more hesitant to voice their doubts.

For most people—and this is where those of us engaged in healing ministry often confront it—the problem of suffering is *personal and experiential*. It's not the unjust suffering in the world that troubles them as much as the unjust suffering they've experienced in their own lives. Deep within them, a confused, raging, angry voice cries out, "God, this isn't fair! Why did you let this happen? What did I do to deserve it? Why did you abandon me? Why weren't you there when I needed you?"

Down through the centuries, Christians have offered a number of different responses to the problem of suffering and evil.[2] But the best response centers on the cross of Christ. As the late Thomas Oden observed, "For classic Christian teaching, the wisest theodicy flows out of a deep reflection upon the cross. There the profound problem of human suffering is transmuted by the even deeper mystery of God's suffering for humanity."[3] How, then, does the cross address the problem of human suffering? And how does that shape our understanding and practice of healing prayer?

GOD FULLY IDENTIFIES WITH HUMAN SUFFERING

The cross tells us in no uncertain terms that God in Christ is one with us in our suffering. In the prophet Isaiah's unforgettable words, Jesus became "a man of sorrows, and acquainted with grief" (Isa. 53:3 KJV). He knew pain and suffering firsthand.

When we suffer, God doesn't stand far off, aloof, and unable or unwilling to get involved. Jesus Christ is Immanuel, God with us. In becoming flesh (John 1:14), the eternal Word of God has fully identified with the human condition. And since suffering is part and parcel of human existence, he experienced suffering throughout his life. But it was during the last twelve hours of his life, from Gethsemane to Golgotha, that his suffering came to a climax. There he personally experienced human suffering in all its ranges.

The late pastoral theologian and psychiatrist Frank Lake said, "It is an astonishing fact that the events of the Crucifixion of Jesus Christ portray every variety of human suffering and evil."[4] He pointed out that on the cross Jesus suffered injustice, felt the shame of nakedness, was deprived of his rights, endured taunting, became the focus of the rage of others, and was rejected and forsaken. In addition, he experienced excruciating physical pain, thirst, hunger, emptiness, torment, confusion, and finally even death itself.[5]

Having personally experienced the breadth and depth of human suffering, Jesus can truly identify with us when we suffer. He is, in philosopher A. N. Whitehead's phrase, "the fellow sufferer who understands." Because Christ "learned obedience from what he suffered" (Heb. 5:8) and has been "touched with the feeling of our infirmities" (Heb. 4:15 KJV), he can empathetically identify with us in our anguish. Acquainted with grief, the man of sorrows can grieve with us and weep with us. Again, in Isaiah's words, "Surely he hath borne our griefs, and carried our sorrows" (Isa. 53:4 KJV).

A university student who Frank Lake had been counseling wrote to him of how this finally dawned on her. Late one night, she was sitting alone in a chapel, railing at God for allowing so much pain and unjust suffering in her life and the lives of others:

I was livid with His apathy. Didn't He *know* what His carelessness had done to us? For the first time in my life I dared to demand an explanation. When none came, I was angrier than I ever remember being. I turned my eyes on to the plain wooden cross and I remembered Calvary. I stood in the crowd which crucified him, hating and despising him. With my own hands I drove the nails into his hands and his feet, and with bursting energy I flogged him and reviled him and spat with nauseated loathing. Now *He* should know what it felt like—to live in the creation He had made. Every breath brought from me the words: "Now You know! Now You know!"

And then I saw something which made my heart stand still. I saw His face, and on it twisted every familiar agony of my own soul. "Now You know" became an awed whisper as I, motionless, watched His agony. "Yes, now I know" was the passionate and pain-filled reply. "Why else should I come?" Stunned, I watched His eyes search desperately for the tiniest flicker of love in mine, and as we faced one another in the bleak and the cold, forsaken by God, frightened and derelict, we loved one another and our pain became silent in the calm.

Nothing can bind us closer than common dereliction for nowhere else is companionship so longed for.[6]

From that moment, this young woman was inseparably bound to Christ. Knowing that Jesus became a man of sorrows and had experienced dereliction like hers didn't resolve all her questions, but it was enough to keep her trusting in God even in the midst of the inexplicable.

Joni Eareckson Tada arrived at a similar conclusion as she reflected on her own tragedy and the tragedy of scores of others. In 1967, when she was seventeen, a tragic diving accident left her a quadriplegic. Yet over the past half century, she has had an incredible, far-reaching ministry through her books, public speaking, television, and work on behalf of the disabled.

Joni receives thousands of letters, and as you would expect, the majority revolve around the problem of suffering. Though she doesn't pretend to have all the answers, she believes that knowing that Jesus suffered on the cross is the greatest key to enduring our suffering and finding healing. As she put it,

> When you are hurting, when your heart is being wrung out like a sponge, when you've just become a quadriplegic, when your husband has just left you, when your son has committed suicide, to try to come up with answers is pointless . . . the only answer that satisfies is to think of that greater affliction—Christ on the cross. And one day he will give us the key that will unlock sense out of it all. But until then, the Man of Sorrows is enough.[7]

Yes, the Man of Sorrows is enough—that is the first crucial part of the Christian response to suffering and evil. It doesn't make our own personal suffering disappear, nor does it solve the age-old enigma of suffering, but it can enable us to keep trusting God even in the presence of the inexplicable. No matter what happens, nothing can separate us from his love. The late John Stott's words get to the heart of it: "I could never myself believe in God if it were not for the cross. . . . In the real world of pain, how could one worship a God who was immune to it? [At the cross] He laid aside his immunity to pain. He entered our world of flesh and blood, tears and death. He suffered for us. Our sufferings become more manageable in the light of his."[8]

CONSIDERING OUR SORROWS IN THE LIGHT OF HIS

Yet many Christians are unaware of this aspect of Christ's work on the cross. They know and understand Christ died for their sins, but they have never been told that on the cross he also bore "[their] griefs, and carried their sorrows" (Isa. 53:4 KJV). In the ministry of healing prayer, particularly in the areas of emotional trauma and brokenness, Jesus wants to use *us* to convey this truth to them. Let's consider some specific ways we might do this.

First, we might encourage them to consider their suffering and affliction, as Joni put it, in the light of "that greater affliction—Christ on the cross." Helping them to reflect on the similarities between their suffering and how Jesus suffered on the cross can be profoundly comforting and healing.

My father, David Seamands, whose healing ministry and classic book *Healing for Damaged Emotions* has touched so many,[9] tells about a situation where he felt led to do this.[10] Two sisters were attending a weekend seminar on emotional and spiritual healing that he was leading. Both had been sexually molested by an uncle and were extremely bitter toward their uncle.

At an afternoon session, they became angry with Dad when he stressed the indispensable part forgiveness plays in healing. Was he suggesting they should forgive their uncle? How could he dare ask them to do that? How could God? Given what their uncle had done to them, didn't they have every right to be resentful and angry?

As far as they were concerned, forgiving him was out of the question. So was trusting God. "You're asking me to trust God?" The older sister exclaimed. "I tried that when I was six years old. I cried out to God to protect me from my uncle, but he didn't. The only thing I could do was cover my head with my pillow."

Wanting to respond sensitively, Dad thanked the sisters for their honest reaction. Then he felt prompted by the Spirit to describe several aspects of Christ's shameful abuse that paralleled theirs. During Jesus's trial, men blindfolded him (the King James Version says they "cover[ed] his face") and beat him with their fists (Mark 14:65). During his crucifixion, he experienced the shame and humiliation of nakedness. That was why in the earliest paintings of the crucifixion, unlike the more recent familiar ones, Jesus always appeared naked.

In hearing this, the older sister felt deeply moved. She never realized Jesus endured these things. It dawned on her that Jesus could identify with her and other victims of sexual abuse. Like her face covered with a pillow, his face had been covered. He, too, must have felt powerless and unprotected by God. She had been stripped of her clothing; so had he. He, too, had shameful indignities inflicted on his naked body.

She realized that Jesus could understand her hurt and anger. He knew why it was so hard for her to forgive her uncle. Jesus did not condemn her for her struggle. He wept for her and with her. He knew firsthand the humiliation she had experienced. On the cross, he bore shame like she had experienced when her uncle molested her.

At the close of the next morning's session, that sister came and knelt to receive prayer for healing. She told my father she was now willing to let go of her bitterness toward her uncle. She also wanted to begin trusting God again. Knowing that Jesus knew, understanding that he understood, broke through her resistance and softened her heart. As she prayed at the altar, bottled-up tears gushed forth, washing away layers of shame. Christ's wounds began to heal hers.

On numerous occasions, as I've engaged in the ministry of healing prayer, I, too, have been led by the Spirit to do something similar. As hurting and broken people have shared their wrenching stories with me, there have been times when I have found myself offering them this invitation: "Come with me and stand beneath the cross of Jesus. Gaze at the bruised and bleeding Son of God hanging there. Reflect on *your* hurts and wounds in the light of *his*."

Hanging in my office is a large picture of Christ on the cross as a visual reminder of his sufferings. I also keep a large wooden crucifix there—one that includes the figure of the suffering Christ. Since touch is often an important element in healing, sometimes I will place the crucifix in the person's hands and encourage them to hold it as they share their deep pain and anguish with me.

Helping people "reframe" the painful picture of their suffering with wood from Calvary's cross can become a significant step in their healing journey. Wonderful things seem to happen when we consider our wounds in the light of his. In most cases, however, it simply isn't appropriate to directly speak of Jesus's suffering on the cross as it relates to theirs. Often we won't have time to do this. So we must communicate that Jesus is a fellow sufferer who understands *without* speaking about it; we must somehow embody this truth without using words.

We can do this through carefully and sensitively listening to their story. Isaiah said, "Surely he hath borne our griefs, and carried our sorrows" (Isa. 53:4 KJV). As we empathically enter their suffering and pain, allowing them to express their anger and disappointment, there is a sense in which, like Jesus, we bear their griefs and carry their sorrows too. And mysteriously, when we do, they seem to sense that Jesus identifies and weeps with them in their suffering.

Yet to be a person who can truly empathize with the suffering of others, we first need to engage our own suffering and pain. When we are still in denial, unwilling to face our own griefs and sorrows, it is difficult to engage the suffering of others. Hearing the story of their suffering will be unsettling and uncomfortable for us.

I know this from my own experience. I was around forty years old before I really connected with the deep aching loneliness in my soul because of long-term separation from my parents associated with attending a missionary boarding school between the ages of seven and twelve. I had been a seminary professor for seven years when I faced that loneliness. And it was only after that, after Jesus walked with me into my pain and began to heal my hurt, that students began knocking on my office door, wanting to talk to me about their deep pain and hurt.

It was as if seeing my own anguish gave me eyes that could see theirs. When I began to feel the emotions buried in my own heart, I could begin to feel theirs. Only after I had wept over my own suffering could I weep with those who weep. To be someone through whom Jesus can convey to others that he is a fellow sufferer who understands, you must come to terms with the suffering in your own life.

GOD'S WAY OF REDEMPTION

The cross tells us that God has fully identified with us in our suffering. He himself, in the person of his Son, suffers with us. He has become a man of sorrows who knows pain and suffering firsthand. He has borne our griefs and carried our sorrows.

But not only does the cross tell us that God is one with us in our suffering; it also tells us that God uses suffering in redeeming creation, in transforming fallen creation to new creation. On the third day, the crucified Jesus was raised from the dead, signifying the beginning of new creation. The Man of Sorrows is now the risen Lord. Henceforth, God is making all things new (Rev. 21:5).

In the Christian scheme of things, God's solution to the problem of suffering and evil is not to eliminate it nor to be insulated from it, but to participate in it, and then having participated in it, to transform it into his instrument for redeeming the world. Simone Weil (1909–43), the French philosopher who converted to Christianity, wrote profoundly about the meaning of suffering and affliction. She expressed it like this: "The extreme greatness of Christianity lies in the fact that it does not seek a supernatural *remedy* for suffering but a supernatural *use* for it."[11]

Christians believe that God uses the suffering and evil of the cross. God weaves it into his redemptive plan and pattern for the salvation of the world. God takes this tragedy and turns it into the triumph of the empty tomb. The grotesque becomes glorious, evil is transmuted into good. Theologian Emil Brunner was right: "If there ever were an event in which evil, innocent suffering, malice and human pain reaches its climax, it is in the cross of Christ."[12] Yet God took the awfulness of that event—the diabolical evil, the flagrant injustice, the excruciating pain—and through a marvelous divine alchemy and the miracle of Christ's resurrection, transformed them into medicine for the healing of the nations.

The cross, then, supremely illustrates the oft-quoted Romans 8:28: "And we know that in all things God works for the good of those who love him, who have been called according to his purpose." It demonstrates that even when things seem to have tragically gone wrong, God can still use anguish creatively to bring out of it blessings that could not have been realized any other way. In fact, this *is* God's method of redemption.

How does God overcome that which opposes his will? How does God demonstrate divine sovereignty and power in the face of evil? Good Friday and Easter Sunday tell us. God accomplishes it through a power that absorbs opposition to God's will through innocent suffering, and then having absorbed the opposition, neutralizes it by forgiving love. Finally, having neutralized evil, God uses it to accomplish the very purpose it was originally designed to thwart.

God overcomes evil, not through passive resignation or brute strength, not through coercion or a dazzling display of force, but through the power of suffering love and resurrection. God uses suffering redemptively to accomplish his will and purpose in the world. That's why, in the Christian scheme of things, even *after* Christ was raised from the dead and given a glorious new resurrection body, the scars in his hands, feet, and side as emblems of his gruesome death, *remain*. God's resurrection power overcame all other evidence of violence done to him. Suffering and death were left behind; he was alive as never before. Yet these marks of humiliation were not erased.

In fact, Jesus's scars became his identifying marks. On that first Easter when his disciples were hiding behind closed doors, he appeared among them and "showed them his hands and side." Then they absolutely knew it was Jesus and were "overjoyed when they saw the Lord" (John 20:20).

The scars were still there—and according to the apostle John, they will *always* be there. Toward the end of his life, when he was given a vision of the throne in heaven, John saw a Lamb standing in the center—a Lamb "looking as if it had been slain" (Rev. 5:6). They are *eternal scars*.

However, now there is one crucial difference: they are *radiant* scars. A verse in the hymn "Crown Him with Many Crowns" conveys this beautifully: "Crown him the Lord of love; behold his hands and side, rich wounds, yet visible above, in beauty glorified."[13] The scars are now bearers of divine glory. The light of God's presence radiates from them, transforming everything it encounters. His scars are now instruments of healing, and as Isaiah prophesied, "By his wounds we are healed" (Isa. 53:5).

RADIANT SCARS AND WOUNDED HEALERS

Such is the wondrous message of the cross for the sufferer. In the face of the wrongs done to us and the suffering we have endured, the cross tells us not only that God in Christ identifies and suffers with us, but that God can take what was meant for evil and use it for good (Gen. 50:20). Our scars can become radiant too. Jesus not only wants to heal our wounds, but like his wounds, he wants ours to become wounds that heal others, marks that signify that new creation has begun.

At a summer camp in Canada where I was speaking, during a time of public sharing, a woman explained how God was teaching her this. "Just a few weeks ago," she began, "my husband and I made a compost pile. We put all sorts of garbage in it—cracked eggshells, darkened banana peels, coffee grounds, piles of rotten leaves and grass—you name it. We mixed it all together and then covered it up. And when you go near it now, believe me, your nose knows it's there! But next spring when we use it in our garden and around our shrubs, what's decaying garbage now will be pure gold. That compost will be so much better than any fertilizer we could buy at the store."

Then she made this application to herself: "There has been lots of garbage in my life—rotten things done to me and rotten things I've done in response. For years I refused to deal with the garbage, but several years ago when my life began to unravel, I was forced to. Thank God for that. As a result, he has worked so much healing and restoration in my life.

"But while all this has been going on, I have often found myself thinking, *I can't wait until this is finally over. I'll be so glad when I can put all the garbage behind me and never have to think about it again. Maybe I'll even be able to pretend it never happened.*

"Then, as we were making the compost pile, the Lord spoke to me: 'All your life you've run from your garbage. Now even though you're finally dealing with it and receiving healing, you're still wanting to run from it. But don't you see? I not only want to heal and free you from its effects in your life; I want to use your garbage. Like the garbage in your compost pile, if you'll let me, I'll turn it into pure gold. I'll use it to build character in you and bring healing and freedom to others.'

"So instead of being ashamed of the garbage, I'm learning to give it to him. And I'm discovering that the Lord is the Great Recycler! He doesn't waste anything. He can turn our garbage into gold—pure gold, if we'll just offer it to Him."

Often in healing prayer ministry, as we walk with people into their places of deep emotional pain and suffering, they are certainly not at a place where they are ready to consider this. At the beginning of the healing process, the last thing they need to hear us say is, "God wants to use this suffering you have experienced for good." Glibly quoting Scripture verses like Romans 8:28 ("In all things God works together for good" [paraphrased]) or Genesis 50:20 ("You meant it for evil, but God meant it for good" [paraphrased]) can do a lot more harm than good. So please don't!

At the beginning of the emotional healing process, the most crucial task is to confront the truth about what happened, embrace the pain, and come to terms with the havoc wreaked by the wrongs done to us. Helping people carefully and honestly survey the damage and lament over what has happened is a crucial, essential part of healing. As the writer of Ecclesiastes reminds us, there is "a time to mourn" (Eccl. 3:4), and that necessary season cannot be rushed or manipulated.

Yet there comes a point toward the end of the emotional healing process when we are called to face our wounds in a different way, this time viewing them not only as enemies but as friends. Strangely, like Paul in relation to his thorn in the flesh (2 Cor. 12:7–10), we can come to *glory* in them because of what they produce in us (weakness) and release through us (God's power). But we need to let people arrive at this conclusion on their own—in their own time and in their own way. It is certainly not our job to force it on them.

In the meantime, however, there is something important we can do. As wounded healers, we can offer ourselves to others as living witnesses of what Christ's healing power can do. When the risen Jesus appeared to doubting Thomas, he invited him to "put your finger here; see my hands. Reach out your hand and put it in my side" (John 20:27). Likewise, when we vulnerably and gently offer ourselves and our wounds to others, we are giving a similar invitation.

By inviting the wounded to touch our wounds, which have become wounds that heal, we are demonstrating and embodying the message of the wondrous cross. We are proclaiming that like Christ's scars, their scars can become radiant too. The very things Satan and the forces of evil wanted to use to destroy them—their places of deepest humiliation, degradation, and shame—Jesus wants to transform and fill with his glorious presence. They can become places of spiritual authority and power.

This, then, is the message of the wondrous cross for the sufferer: Jesus's scars have become radiant; he can make our scars radiant too. Regarding Jesus's scars, Charles Wesley wrote beautifully in "Lo! He Comes with Clouds Descending," his great hymn about the second coming of Christ,

> Those dear tokens of his passion
> still his dazzling body bears,
> cause of endless exultation
> to his ransomed worshipers.
> With what rapture,
> with what rapture,
> with what rapture,
> gaze we on those glorious scars![14]

And regarding our scars, a statement often attributed to Augustine declares, "In my deepest wound I saw your glory, and it dazzled me."[15]

EIGHT

THE HOLY SPIRIT AND HEALING

Throughout this book, I have stressed that the healing ministry of Jesus Christ didn't end when he ascended to heaven. It continues on earth today through his body, the church. Our healing ministry is a participation in the ongoing healing ministry of Jesus Christ. We are called not to lead but to follow the Healer.

However, to this point I have not answered a crucial, all-important question: How? The Apostles' Creed says, regarding Jesus, that "he ascended into heaven and sits at the right hand of God." How, then, do we, who are here on earth, join with Jesus, who is ascended and is there in heaven? This all-important question is the focus of this final chapter.

We can answer that question in four words: through the

Holy Spirit. It's as simple—and as complex—as that! We are joined to the risen, ascended Jesus and participate in his ongoing healing ministry through the person and work of the Holy Spirit. The Holy Spirit, the third person of the Trinity, is the one who connects us to Christ the Son and makes healing ministry—in fact, all Christian ministry—possible. This is why at the end of his earthly ministry, knowing that he would soon be departing, Jesus intentionally began to teach his disciples about the work of the Holy Spirit. He knew what a vital and essential role the Spirit would soon play in their lives.

The heart of Jesus's teaching is contained in his Upper Room Discourse, found in chapters 13–17 of John's gospel. Here, for the first time, Jesus referred to the Holy Spirit with a unique personal name: Paraclete. No English word is comprehensive enough to grasp the full meaning of that Greek word,[1] so biblical scholars use various words (e.g., "Comforter" [KJV]; "Advocate" [NIV, NSRV]; "Counselor" [CSB]; "Helper" [ESV]) when translating it into English. In his teaching, Jesus made it clear that the Paraclete is distinct from himself. Though he was going away, he told his disciples, the Paraclete, who is "another advocate," would come to be with them forever (John 14:16). At the same time, however, the Paraclete is inseparable from Jesus. Though they are not the same, there is a unique, indivisible relationship between them. For example, Jesus told his disciples, "When the [Paraclete] comes, whom I will send to you from the Father . . . he will testify *on my behalf*"

(John 15:26 NRSV, emphasis added). He also said, "He [the Paraclete] will glorify me, because he will take what is mine and declare it to you" (John 16:14 NRSV). And earlier he insisted, "This is the Spirit of truth. . . . You know him, because he abides with you, and he will be in you. I will not leave you orphaned; *I am coming to you*" (John 14:17–18 NRSV, emphasis added).

New Testament scholar Raymond Brown included a meticulous ten-page study on the meaning of *Paraclete* in his two-volume commentary on the Gospel of John. He concluded that when Jesus called the Holy Spirit the Paraclete, he meant "the Holy Spirit in a special role, namely, as *the personal presence of Jesus in the Christian while Jesus is with the Father.*"[2] Through the Holy Spirit, the Paraclete, we are personally joined with our ascended Lord. Jesus is both in heaven at the right hand of the Father and, through the Holy Spirit, personally present in us! In considering what happened on the day of Pentecost, we can easily get preoccupied with the wind, fire, and speaking in tongues—the three external signs present when the Holy Spirit was poured out on those gathered in the upper room (Acts 2:1–4). But above all, when the Holy Spirit was poured out upon the disciples, the personal presence of the risen, ascended Christ came to dwell in them and abide with them.

In describing what happened on the day of Pentecost, the great Bible teacher and expositor G. Campbell Morgan (1863–1945) wrote:

Then what was new as the result of the coming of the Spirit? Comprehensively, by that whelming of the Spirit, these [men and women], disciples, friends, servants . . . were made actually, though mystically one with Him in the very fact of His own life. They were made sharers of the life of the Christ. They had never been that before. . . .

When the Spirit came, His actual life passed into their lives. . . . In half an hour after Pentecost they knew more about Jesus Christ than they had ever known before. . . .

Were they no longer His servants? Surely His servants, but no longer sent from Him, but the very instruments of His own going. Their hands became His hands to touch [others] tenderly; their feet, His feet to run on swift errands of God's love; their eyes His eyes, to flame with His tenderness; themselves part of Himself.[3]

When the Holy Spirit came upon these early believers, Jesus himself—the risen, ascended Jesus, seated at the Father's right hand—came alive in them. Through the Holy Spirit they were now connected to the person of Jesus, to his character and his ministry. That's why several times in the New Testament, the Holy Spirit is even referred to as the Spirit of Christ (Acts 16:7; Gal. 4:6; 1 Peter 1:11). His very life was in them, so much so that Paul could even say, "I no longer live, but Christ lives in me" (Gal. 2:20). And because Christ himself was in them, they were being conformed to his own image and likeness (Rom. 8:29). Through the Holy Spirit, the *character* of Jesus was being formed in them. And through the Spirit, the *ministry* of Jesus was also continuing through them. No longer were they merely set apart by him and commissioned for ministry. Rather, as Morgan put it, they became "the very instruments of His own going." Through the Holy Spirit, Jesus—risen, ascended, and seated at God's right hand—was now carrying out his ministry through them. Through them, Jesus was continuing to preach, teach, and *heal.*

Let's consider the work of the Holy Spirit in connecting us to both the character of Jesus and the ministry of Jesus, especially as it relates to healing ministry.

THE FRUIT OF THE SPIRIT AND THE CHARACTER OF JESUS

In Galatians 5:16–26, the apostle Paul contrasted the sinful works of the flesh with the fruit the Holy Spirit produces in us: "By contrast, the fruit of the Spirit is love, joy, peace, patience, kindness, generosity, faithfulness, gentleness, and self-control" (Gal. 5:22–23 NRSV). According to John Stott, this cluster of nine moral virtues seems to comprehensively portray a Christian's attitude toward God (love, joy, peace), others (patience, kindness, generosity), and self (faithfulness, gentleness, and self-control).[4] Above all, they paint a beautiful, comprehensive portrait of Christlikeness. As New Testament scholar Gordon Fee observed, "The essential nature of the fruit is the reproduction of the life of Christ in the life of the believer."[5] Likewise, according to Craig Keener, "The fruit of the Spirit is the character of the Spirit of God's Son living in us."[6]

We usually associate healing ministry with the *gifts* of the Spirit, not the *fruit* of the Spirit. But before we discuss the vital role spiritual gifts do play in healing, let me tell you why the fruit of the Spirit, or growth in Christlike character, is so important in the lives of those involved in healing ministry.

In the Sermon on the Mount, Jesus emphasized that "the eye is the lamp of the body. So, if your eye is healthy, your whole body will be full of light, but if your eye is unhealthy, your whole body will be full of darkness. If, then, the light in you is darkness, how great is the darkness!" (Matt. 6:22–23 NRSV). According to Jesus, our spiritual vision and insight, our capacity to discern and understand, depends on a "healthy" eye that is "full of light." Unhealthy eyes, which are a mixture of light and darkness, result in vision that is dim, blurry, and opaque.

Much of what happens in healing ministry depends on our ability to see. When we properly understand and discern someone's true needs, we will then know how to pray for them. This is why growth and maturity in Christlike character in us, through the growth and maturing of the fruit of the Spirit, is so vital. The more light and the less darkness in us, the more personally integrated and less internally divided we are and the better we can understand and perceive the healing needs of others.

Thomas à Kempis, the writer of the great Christian classic *The Imitation of Christ*, expressed the concept like this: "The more [we] are made one with [ourselves], and simple in heart, the more and deeper matters and without effort [we] comprehend, because [we] receive the light of understanding from above."[7] That's exactly what happens as the fruit of the Spirit ripens in us and we grow up into maturity in Christ. The more single and undivided we are, the easier it is to hear Christ's voice, discern his will, and penetrate with his vision into the hearts of others.

We also will become persons others can trust and feel comfortable with. The more the fruit of the Spirit ripens in us, the more content and less anxious we will be, and the more safe and secure others will feel around us. The more we are transformed into Christ's likeness, the more they will be drawn to the unanxious presence of Jesus dwelling in us. And that—in and of itself—can be profoundly healing.

THE GIFTS OF THE SPIRIT AND THE MINISTRY OF JESUS

The Holy Spirit is on a mission to make us more like Jesus and to cause his *character* to be deeply formed in us. But the Holy Spirit is also on a mission to draw us into the ongoing *ministry* of Jesus. This happens through the impartation of the gifts of the Holy Spirit in us.

Much has been written about spiritual gifts in the last

fifty years.[8] Simply defined, spiritual gifts are special abilities for Christian service given by the Holy Spirit through which Jesus works to strengthen, build up, and empower his body, the church. In the New Testament there are four key passages—all found in Paul's letters—where various gifts of the Spirit are listed (Rom. 12:6–8; 1 Cor. 12:8–10; 12:28–31; Eph. 4:7–12). To be sure, the gifts mentioned in these passages are meant to be representative, not exhaustive. Nowhere is Paul attempting to compile a complete list of every gift given by the Holy Spirt. In each case, he only mentions some, in keeping with the particular subject matter and focus of his letter.

All the gifts are vital and needed in the life of the church. That's why Paul exhorted us to "follow the way of love and *eagerly desire* gifts of the Spirit" (1 Cor. 14:1, emphasis added). Of the twenty-one gifts mentioned in these four passages, the following are particularly important for healing ministry: prophecy (Rom. 12:6; 1 Cor. 12:10, 29; Eph. 4:11), encouragement (Rom. 12:8), mercy (Rom. 12:8), word of wisdom (1 Cor. 12:8), word of knowledge (1 Cor. 12:8), faith (1 Cor. 12:9), healing (1 Cor. 12:9, 28), working of miracles (1 Cor. 12:10, 29), and discernment of spirits (1 Cor. 12:10). Sometimes these have been referred to as "the healing gifts of the Spirit."

Although these gifts are not explicitly defined in the New Testament, if you read the various books written about spiritual gifts, you'll find helpful tentative definitions in many of them. The late Dr. Kenneth Kinghorn, my seminary teacher and later faculty colleague at Asbury Theological Seminary for many years, taught and wrote several excellent books on spiritual gifts. Here are the definitions he offers in *The New Testament Gifts of the Holy Spirit*:

- Prophecy—applying the biblical revelation with clarity and power as light and truth for the present
- Encouragement—comforting and encouraging others, using the ministries of sympathetic understanding and scriptural counsel to cause right attitudes and actions
- Mercy—sensing needs in others, feeling sympathy, and cheerfully showing compassion and giving comfort
- Word of wisdom—receiving a Spirit-assisted illumination that enables one to understand and share the mind of the Holy Spirit in a specific circumstance
- Word of knowledge—knowing a fact or circumstance based on direct illumination by the Holy Spirit
- Faith—the Spirit-given ability to believe that because God is able to do wonderful works, we can trust him to bring them to pass in response to prayer and faith
- Healing—praying prayers of faith that bring God's healing to sick, frail, or disordered bodies, souls, and relationships

- Miracles—trusting God to work supernaturally in people and circumstances, especially by healing, freeing from evil spirits, and delivering from dangers
- Discernment of spirits—sensing whether a teacher or proposed action comes from a divine source, a human source, or an evil source.[9]

Now, I'm not suggesting that to be involved in healing ministry you must operate in *all* of these gifts. But those who are drawn to and regularly involved in healing ministry will generally operate in *some* of them. This is one of the primary reasons I prefer to engage in healing prayer with a team of people (myself along with one or two others). The other members of the team often will operate in gifts that I don't generally operate in and vice versa. When there is a wider range of healing gifts present, as a team we are able to minister to someone much more fruitfully and effectively.

How do these particular gifts of the Spirit relate to the ongoing healing ministry of Jesus? Think of it like this: the healing gifts of the Spirit enable us to *feel* with the *heart* of Jesus (mercy), *see* with the *eyes* of Jesus (word of wisdom, word of knowledge, discernment of Spirits), *speak* with the *mouth* of Jesus (prophecy, encouragement, faith), and *touch* with the *hands* of Jesus (healing, miracles). Through these gifts which the Holy Spirit bestows upon us "as he determines" (1 Cor. 12:11), the risen, ascended Jesus in heaven continues his ministry of healing to people on earth.

This means that we should pray for the anointing of the

Holy Spirit and the impartation of the healing gifts of the Spirit as we minister to people. Without the anointing and gifting of the Spirit and left to our own human resources and abilities, we will never be able to get the job done. The apostle Paul exhorted young Timothy to "fan into flame the gift of God, which is in you" (2 Tim. 1:6). Pray then, that the gifts the Spirit has bestowed upon you would be fanned into flame for the sake of those who need Christ's healing touch.

We should also work in stewarding and developing the gifts we have been given. In Jesus's parable of the talents (Matt. 25:14–30; Luke 19:11–27), that's what the master commended the two good and faithful servants for doing. They invested what they had been given, and it multiplied.

So, as you discover your spiritual gifts, you should study and learn all you can about them, read books about them, attend workshops and seminars, and find out about the pitfalls associated with them. Above all, seek out people who are similarly gifted—especially those who are wiser and more experienced than you. Ask them if they would be willing to mentor you.

THE HOLY SPIRIT IN JESUS'S MINISTRY AND OURS

Are you beginning to grasp the vital, indispensable role the Holy Spirit plays in healing ministry? Without the Holy

Spirit working in us, cultivating fruit and bestowing gifts, the healing ministry of Jesus through us will not happen. It's as plain and simple as that.

In fact, without the Holy Spirit's working, Jesus himself would have been unable to carry out his own earthly ministry. Throughout his ministry, he depended on the Holy Spirit, who descended upon him when he was baptized in the Jordan by John (Luke 3:21–22) and remained on him (John 1:33) throughout his life. It is significant that Jesus does no mighty works, no works of healing, prior to the Holy Spirit's coming upon him.

Of course, Jesus had a relationship with the Holy Spirit from the moment of his conception. In the words of the Apostles' Creed, he was "conceived by the Holy Spirit." But something happened to him on the day of his baptism—a filling and anointing of the Spirit—which caused that relationship to deepen and expand. The late theologian Colin Gunton suggested that Jesus "entered a new form of relationship with the Spirit."[10] Consequently, Jesus, being "full of the Holy Spirit" (Luke 4:1) was able to overcome temptation in the wilderness (Luke 4:1–13) and then go forth to preach, teach, and heal with authority and power. As he declared in the synagogue in Nazareth, his hometown, quoting the words of the prophet Isaiah, "The Spirit of the Lord is on me, because he has anointed me to proclaim good news to the poor . . . to proclaim freedom for the prisoners and recovery of sight for the blind" (Luke 4:18).

Later the apostle Peter, as he preached to the Gentiles

in the house of Cornelius, would emphasize "how God anointed Jesus of Nazareth with the Holy Spirit and power" and "how [Jesus] went around doing good and healing all who were under the power of the devil" (Acts 10:38). There is simply no way to account for Jesus's own healing ministry apart from his relationship to the Holy Spirit.

The same holds true for the leaders of the apostolic church. The risen Christ instructed them to wait for the outpouring of the promised Holy Spirit (Luke 24:49; Acts 1:4–8) before attempting to engage in his work. Ten days later, on the day of Pentecost, they were all "filled with the Holy Spirit" (Acts 2:4) and began to minister in boldness and power and authority to heal. Throughout Acts, Luke described various church leaders as being filled with the Holy Spirit (4:8; 6:3, 5; 7:55; 9:17; 11:24; 13:9) as though it were an essential requirement for ministry. Of course, this begs the question: if it was an essential requirement for them, is it not also for us too?

What does it mean to be filled with the Holy Spirit? Although it is a spatial metaphor, being filled with the Spirit is not really about space—like filling up a cup with water. Essentially, this metaphor describes a deeper form of relationship with the Holy Spirit characterized by surrender and abandonment to the Spirit, which deepens and expands our love for God and others. Of course all believers have a relationship with the Holy Spirit. At conversion they "receive the gift of the Holy Spirit" (Acts 2:38) and are "born of the Spirit" (John 3:5–8). Yet the Holy Spirit, though present in all believers, is not preeminent. Though *resident* in all, the Spirit is not *president*. That is why Paul exhorts believers who have already been "sealed" with the Spirit and have a relationship with the Holy Spirit (Eph. 1:13) to be filled with the Holy Spirit (Eph. 5:18). When that happens, we are drawn into both the character of Jesus (fruits of the Spirit) and ministry of Jesus (gifts of the Spirit) in a deeper, richer, more powerful, expansive way.

BE FILLED WITH THE SPIRIT

I conclude this final chapter by inviting you to be filled with the Spirit. Many people I have personally known, and many who have written about healing, also stress the necessity of being filled with the Spirit. In fact, they will often point to their own deeper experience of the Spirit's fullness as the point when they began to experience a passion and an anointing for healing ministry they had never known before.

I'll never forget when this happened in my own life. I was in my late thirties and was at a point where I was becoming increasingly dissatisfied with the level of fruitfulness and power I was experiencing in ministry. Others might have thought I was doing quite well since I was a professor of theology at Asbury Theological Seminary. But I wasn't satisfied. So often I felt unable to "get the job done" in ministering to others so as to bring them into the presence of Christ.

At the time, in addition to teaching at the seminary, I was pastoring a small rural church on weekends. One Sunday I was driving home after leading worship, feeling very discouraged and defeated. Suddenly I burst into tears. "Jesus," I cried, "there's got to be more than this. I want to know more of you—more of your character and more of your ministry. I want to truly know what it means to partner with you as you minister to others through me."

In my anguish, the Lord came and encouraged me. "Steve," he whispered, "you're like a pilot in a small two-seater airplane trying to take off. You get the plane a few feet off the ground, but then you sputter, lose power, and fall back down on the runway. But don't quit—keep pressing in. Don't be discouraged. I want to do more for you. Steve, I'm going to teach you to fly, and someday you're going to soar like an eagle."

About a year later, what Jesus spoke to me that Sunday began to come true. He got me off the runway, and I began to learn how to fly. Ever since, I have experienced a level of adventure, power, and fruitfulness in ministry I had never known before. It became less and less about *my* ministry and more and more, through the Holy Spirit, about joining Jesus in *his* ministry. That's what led me into the ministry of healing.

Over the last decade, I've been discovering more about "soaring like an eagle." I'm learning that, like an eagle, I only have to spread my wings—not flap them—and the wind of the Spirit will buoy me up and do the rest. I'm learning to arise and minister out of his rest, which is so much more powerful than our work.

If Jesus is calling you to join him in his healing ministry, he wants to fill you with the Holy Spirit and anoint you so he can accomplish his ministry through you. Right now, however, he may be calling you to do what the disciples did prior to Pentecost—to wait and devote yourself to prayer until you are endued with power from on high.

The great missionary E. Stanley Jones often said that "unless the Holy Spirit fills, the human spirit fails."[11] Perhaps, like me, some of your recent failures in your efforts to serve Christ have made you painfully aware of that. As never before, you realize that without the Holy Spirit, you will never be able to join Jesus in the healing ministry he is calling you to. Like the disciples, then, you need to tarry and wait. You need to ask the risen, ascended Christ to send the Holy Spirit upon you and fill you. If so, don't be in a hurry. Devote yourself to prayer. Find others who will pray with you. Walk in obedience. Search your heart. As you pray, ask Jesus to increase three things in you.

First, ask him to increase your *desire* for more of himself and more of the fullness of the Holy Spirit. "Before we can be filled with the Spirit," wrote A. W. Tozer, "*the desire to be filled must be all consuming* . . . The degree of fullness in any life accords perfectly with the intensity of true desire. We have as much of God as we actually want."[12] In speaking about the Spirit, Jesus himself said, "Let anyone who is *thirsty* come to me and drink" (John 7:37, emphasis added).

Ask the Lord Jesus to make you thirsty by increasing your desire for more of the Holy Spirit.

Second, ask Jesus to increase your will to surrender and give up control. Richard Neuhaus was right: "It is our determination to be independent by being in control that makes us unavailable to God."[13] To experience more of the Spirit's presence in our lives, we need to surrender areas of our lives where we are insisting on being "independent by being in control." Where in your life does self need to be dethroned and Christ enthroned? And do you have areas of unhealed hurt and pain in your life where you are holding on to anger, bitterness, and unforgiveness? Ask the Lord to empty you of anything preventing the Holy Spirit from being in control. Ask him to increase your will to surrender all to him.

Third, ask Jesus to increase your faith in his promise and the heavenly Father's promise to give you the Holy Spirit. Jesus described this promise of the Father's when he said, "If you then, though you are evil, know how to give good gifts to your children, how much more will your Father in heaven give the Holy Spirit to those who ask him!" (Luke 11:13). In asking him to fill us with his Holy Spirit, we can be confident that the Father wants to give more than we want to receive. The Father will give the Holy Spirit to those who ask him. We don't have to overcome his stinginess or reluctance to fill us with the Spirit. We just need to take hold of his willingness to give.

And Christ the Son's willingness too! He himself told the disciples, "It is for your good that I'm going away. . . .

If I go, I will send [the Holy Spirit] to you" (John 16:7). "I am going to send you what my Father has promised" (Luke 24:49). When Jesus ascended, he was exalted to the place where he joined the Father in sending the Holy Spirit. As Peter declared in his Pentecost sermon, "Exalted to the right hand of God, he has received from the Father the promised Holy Spirit and has poured out what you now see and hear" (Acts 2:33).

The heart of the Father longs for you to experience the person, power, and presence of the Holy Spirit. And the Son, through his life, death, resurrection, and ascension, has accomplished everything necessary for that to happen. Ask that your faith and confidence in the Father and Son's promise to pour out the Spirit on you will increase. Stand on their promises.

Devote yourself to prayer as the disciples did. Ask the ascended Christ to send the Holy Spirit upon you so you can join him in participating in his healing ministry. Ask him to intensify your desire, deepen your surrender, and increase your faith.

Persevere in prayer. Cry out like Jacob did as he wrestled all night with the angel, "I will not let you go unless you bless me" (Gen. 32:26). You can be confident the Lord Jesus will bless you if you do. He will give you the Holy Spirit. He will bless you so that as he carries out his healing ministry through you, you will truly become a blessing to others.

NOTES

CHAPTER 1: PARTICIPATING IN THE HEALING MINISTRY OF JESUS

1. Stephen Seamands, *Wounds That Heal: Bringing Our Hurts to the Cross* (Downers Grove, IL: InterVarsity Press, 2003).
2. Simon Sinek, *Start with Why: How Great Leaders Inspire Everyone to Take Action* (London: Penguin, 2009), 70 (emphasis original).
3. John R. W. Stott, *The Message of Acts* (Downers Grove, IL: InterVarsity Press, 1990), 34.
4. I wrote about this in *The Unseen Real* (Franklin, TN: Seedbed, 2016).
5. Mother Teresa, *The Joy in Loving* (New York: Penguin Compass), 1996.
6. Leanne Payne, *The Healing Presence* (Westchester, IL: Crossway, 1989), xv–xvi.
7. Brad Long and Cindy Strickler, *Let Jesus Heal Your Hidden Wounds* (Grand Rapids: Chosen, 2001), 37.

CHAPTER 2: HEALING AND THE LOVE OF JESUS

1. C. S. Lewis, *The Magician's Nephew* (New York: Collier, 1955), 142.
2. Lewis, 164.
3. See the fine discussion of this word in William Barclay,

New Testament Words (London: SCM, 1964), 276–80. For a more recent discussion, see F. Scott Spencer, *Passions of the Christ* (Grand Rapids: Baker Academic, 2021), 184–90.

4. Ken Blue, *Authority to Heal* (Downers Grove, IL: InterVarsity Press, 1987), 78.
5. Raniero Cantalamessa, *Come, Creator Spirit* (Collegeville, MN: Liturgical Press, 2003), 198.
6. Dan Wilt, *Receive the Holy Spirit* (Franklin, TN: Seedbed, 2022), 113.
7. Wilt, 114.
8. Tilda Norberg, *Consenting to Grace: An Introduction to Gestalt Pastoral Care* (Staten Island, NY: Penn House, 2006), 38–39.
9. Oswald Chambers, *If Ye Shall Ask* (New York: Dodd, Mead, 1938), 47.
10. Lewis, *Magician's Nephew*, 164.
11. Charles Wesley, "Love Divine, All Loves Excelling," Hymnary.org, https://hymnary.org/text/love_divine_all_love_excelling_joy_of_he. Public domain (1747).
12. John Wesley, "Primitive Physic," in *The Works of John Wesley*, vol. 32, *Medical and Health Writings*, ed. James Donat and Randy Maddox (Nashville: Abingdon, 2018), 119.

CHAPTER 3: THE FIVE WAYS JESUS HEALS

1. Amanda Porterfield, *Healing in the History of Christianity* (New York: Oxford University Press, 2005), 3.
2. I first heard Dr. Frank Bateman Stanger formally talk about the five miracles of healing. I believe he had derived and adapted them from E. Stanley Jones's teaching on healing. They are briefly presented in Donald Demaray, *Experiencing Healing and Wholeness* (Indianapolis: Light and Life, 1999), 178–79.
3. Francis MacNutt, *The Healing Reawakening* (Grand Rapids: Chosen, 2005).

4. Candy Gunther Brown, *Global Pentecostal and Charismatic Healing* (New York: Oxford University Press, 2011), 3.
5. Craig S. Keener, *Miracles: The Credibility of the New Testament Accounts*, 2 vols. (Grand Rapids: Baker Academic, 2011).
6. Craig S. Keener, *Miracles Today: The Supernatural Work of God in the Modern World* (Grand Rapids: Baker Academic, 2021).
7. Porterfield, *Healing in the History of Christianity*, 141.
8. Michael Brown, *Israel's Divine Healer* (Grand Rapids: Zondervan, 1995), 238.
9. Brown, 239.
10. Porterfield, *Healing in the History of Christianity*, 141–58.
11. Porterfield, 141.
12. Allen Verhey, *The Christian Art of Dying* (Grand Rapids: Eerdmans, 2011), 309–10.
13. Demaray, *Experiencing Healing and Wholeness*, 179.
14. Paul Tournier, *A Doctor's Casebook in the Light of the Bible* (New York: Harper & Row, 1960), 149–50.
15. In the discussion of Paul's thorn in the flesh, I have adapted material from my book *Wounds That Heal: Bringing Our Hurts to the Cross* (Downers Grove, IL: InterVarsity Press, 2003), 171–73.
16. Raniero Cantalamessa, *Come, Creator Spirit* (Collegeville, MN: Liturgical Press, 2003), 281.
17. Peter Kreeft, *Heaven: The Heart's Deepest Longing* (San Francisco: Ignatius, 1980), 234.
18. 15 August 1750, *The Works of John Wesley*, vol. 20, *Journals and Diaries IV*, ed. W. Reginald Ward and Richard P. Heitzenrater (Nashville: Abingdon, 1991), 356.
19. Robert Webster, *Methodism and the Miraculous* (Lexington, KY: Emeth, 2013), 12.
20. John Wesley, *The Works of John Wesley*, vol. 4, ed. Thomas Jackson (Grand Rapids: Zondervan), 496.
21. John Wesley, *The Works of John Wesley*, vol. 9, *The*

Methodist Societies: History, Nature, and Design, ed. Rupert Davies (Nashville: Abingdon, 1989), 275.

22. Letter to Lady Maxwell (23 February 1767) in *The Letters of the Rev. John Wesley, A.M.*, ed. John Telford (London: Epworth, 1931), 5:42.

23. 12 May 1759, The *Works of John Wesley*, vol. 21, *Journals and Diaries IV*, ed. W. Reginald Ward and Richard P. Heitzenrater (Nashville: Abingdon, 1992), 191.

24. John Wesley, *The Works of John Wesley*, vol. 32, *Medical and Health Writings*, ed. James G. Donat and Randy L. Maddox (Nashville: Abingdon, 2018), 119.

25. John Wesley, *The Works of John Wesley*, vol. 7, *A Collection of Hymns for the Use of the People Called Methodist*, ed. Franz Hildebrandt and Oliver Beckerlegge (Nashville: Abingdon, 1983), 476.

26. Letter to Mrs. Woodhouse (17 May 1766) in *The Letters of the Rev. John Wesley, A.M.*, ed. John Telford (London: Epworth, 1931), 5:12.

27. John Fanestil, *Mrs. Hunter's Happy Death* (New York: Doubleday, 2006).

28. Quoted in E. Brooks Holifield, *Health and Medicine in the Methodist Tradition* (New York: Crossroad, 1986), 89.

29. See Joseph D. McPherson, *"Our People Die Well"* (Bloomington, IN: AuthorHouse, 2008).

30. Chris Johnson, "Dying Well according to John Wesley," Seedbed, April 17, 2012, https://seedbed.com/dying-well -according-to-john-wesley.

CHAPTER 4: HEALING AND THE IMAGE OF GOD

1. Ray S. Anderson, *On Becoming Human* (Grand Rapids: Eerdmans, 1982), 70.

2. Nonna Harrison, *God's Many-Splendored Image* (Grand Rapids: Baker Academic, 2010), 5.

3. Cornelius Plantinga Jr., "Images of God," in *Christian Faith*

& *Practice in the Modern World*, ed. Mark Noll and David Wells (Grand Rapids: Eerdmans, 1988), 52.

4. Anthony Hoekema, *Created in God's Image* (Grand Rapids: Eerdmans, 1986), 70–71.
5. This is similar to what theologian Stanley Grenz and Christian psychologist Todd Hall advocate. See Stanley Grenz, *The Social God and the Relational Self* (Louisville, KY: Westminister John Knox, 2001), 177–82; and Todd W. Hall *Relational Spirituality: A Psychological-Theological Paradigm for Transformation* (Downers Grove, IL: InterVarsity Press, 2021), 65–70.
6. John Wesley, "A Further Appeal to Men of Reason and Religion," pt. 1, para. 3, in *The Works of John Wesley*, vol. 11, *The Appeals to Men of Reason and Religion*, ed. Gerald R. Cragg (Oxford: Clarendon, 1975), 106.
7. John Wesley, "Original Sin," in *The Works of John Wesley*, vol. 2, *Sermons II*, ed. Albert C. Outler (Nashville: Abingdon, 1985), 185.
8. Frank Bateman Stanger, *God's Healing Community* (Nashville: Abingdon, 1978), 26.
9. John J. Pilch, *Healing in the New Testament* (Minneapolis: Fortress, 2000), 59.
10. Pilch, 59.
11. William Barclay, *And He Had Compassion* (Valley Forge, PA: Judson, 1976), 47.

CHAPTER 5: JESUS, HEALING, AND THE KINGDOM OF GOD

1. Jürgen Moltmann, *The Source of Life*, trans. Margaret Kohl (London: SCM, 1997), 64.
2. George Eldon Ladd, *The Gospel of the Kingdom* (Grand Rapids: Eerdmans, 1959), 48.
3. Gordon Fee, *Paul, the Spirit, and the People of God* (Peabody, MA: Hendrickson, 1996), 51.

4. Fee, 146.
5. See Amanda Porterfield, *Healing in the History of Christianity* (Oxford: Oxford University Press, 2005); and Francis MacNutt, *The Healing Reawakening* (Grand Rapids: Chosen, 2005).
6. See Candy Gunther Brown, ed., *Global Pentecostal and Charismatic Healing* (New York: Oxford University Press, 2011); Craig S. Keener, *Miracles: The Credibility of the New Testament Accounts*, 2 vols. (Grand Rapids: Baker Academic, 2011).
7. For an excellent rebuttal to the various cessationist arguments, see Jack Deere, *Surprised by the Power of the Spirit* (Grand Rapids: Zondervan, 1993), 223–52. See also his recent reworking of this book, *Why I Am Still Surprised by the Spirit* (Grand Rapids: Zondervan Reflective, 2020).
8. Ken Blue, *Authority to Heal* (Downers Grove, IL: InterVarsity Press, 1987), 115.
9. Derek Morphew, *Breakthrough: Discovering the Kingdom* (Cape Town, South Africa: Vineyard International, 2006), 88.
10. George Eldon Ladd, *A Theology of the New Testament* (Grand Rapids: Eerdmans, 1974), 76.
11. Morphew, *Breakthrough*, 88.
12. Albert Day, *Letters on the Healing Ministry* (Nashville: Abingdon, 1986), 52.
13. Forgiveness is a complicated issue, and forgiving others often involves a slow process. Those who engage in healing prayer should learn all they can about it. I wrote a chapter about it in my book *Wounds That Heal: Bringing Our Hurts to the Cross* (Downers Grove, IL: InterVarsity Press, 2003), 130–47.

CHAPTER 6: EMBRACING THE MYSTERY OF HEALING

1. Bennett Cerf, Donald Klopper, and Robert Haas, eds., *The Poems and Plays of Alfred Lord Tennyson* (New York: Random House, 1938), 721.

2. Catechism of the Catholic Church, quoted in Michael Downey, *Altogether Gift: A Trinitarian Spirituality* (Maryknoll, NY: Orbis, 200), 40.
3. Ken Blue, *Authority to Heal* (Downers Grove, IL: InterVarsity Press, 1987), 40.
4. Francis MacNutt, *The Power to Heal* (Notre Dame, IN: Ave Maria, 1977), 62.
5. For more in-depth study of this issue, see the following articles: John Wilkinson, "Physical Healing and the Atonement," *Evangelical Quarterly* 63, no. 2 (1991): 149–67; and Graham Hill, "The Atonement and Healing: Is Physical Healing Guaranteed in Jesus's Death on the Cross?," The GlobalChurch Project, April 17, 2016, https://theglobalchurchproject.com/atonement-healing-wrestling-contemporary-issue/.
6. Jürgen Moltmann, *The Spirit of Life* (Minneapolis: Fortress, 1992), 191.
7. Sam Storms, "Does Matthew 8 Teach Healing in the Atonement?," June 21, 2021, https://www.thegospelcoalition.org/article/physical-healing-atonement/, emphasis original.
8. An insightful discussion of this issue can be found in Ken Blue, *Authority to Heal*, 41–51, 97–105.
9. Randy Clark, *Power to Heal* (Shippensburg, PA: Destiny Image, 2015), 227.
10. Clark, 227.
11. Clark, 227–44.
12. Clark, 234.
13. Keith Warrington, *Jesus the Healer* (Waynesboro, GA: Paternoster, 2000), 27.
14. Blue, *Authority to Heal*, 104.

CHAPTER 7: BY HIS WOUNDS WE ARE HEALED

1. Quoted in Jurgen Moltmann, *The Crucified God* (New York: Harper & Row, 1974), 220.

2. Thomas Oden outlined twelve such Christian responses. He called them "pastoral consolations." See the chapter "A Theodicy for Pastoral Practice" in his *Pastoral Theology: Essentials for Ministry* (San Francisco: Harper and Row, 1983), 223–48.
3. Thomas Oden, *Classic Christianity* (New York: HarperOne, 2009), 436.
4. Frank Lake, *Clinical Theology: A Theological and Psychiatric Basis to Clinical Pastoral Care* (London: Darton, Longman & Todd, 1966), 18.
5. For an informative description of the various ways Jesus suffered on the cross, see Thomas W. McGovern, *What Christ Suffered: A Doctor's Journey through the Passion* (Huntington, IN: Our Sunday Visitor, 2021).
6. Lake, *Clinical Theology*, 820–21.
7. Joni Eareckson Tada, *Christian Counseling Connection*, vol. 3, ed. Gary Collins (Glen Ellyn, IL: Christian Counseling Resources, 1999).
8. John R. W. Stott, *The Cross of Christ* (Downers Grove, IL: InterVarsity Press, 1986), 335–36.
9. David Seamands's book *Healing for Damaged Emotions* (Wheaton, IL: David C. Cook, 2015) has been translated into more than thirty-five languages and has sold over a million copies.
10. Stephen Seamands, *Wounds That Heal: Bringing Our Hurts to the Cross* (Downers Grove, IL: InterVarsity Press, 2003), 50–51.
11. Simone Weil, *Gravity and Grace* (London: Routledge & Kegan Paul, 1952), 73.
12. Emil Brunner, *The Christian Doctrine of Creation and Redemption* (Philadelphia: Westminster, 1952), 181.
13. Matthew Bridges and Godfrey Thring, "Crown Him with Many Crowns," Hymnary.org, https://hymnary.org/text/crown_him_with_many_crowns. Public domain (1871).

14. Charles Wesley, "Lo! He Comes with Clouds Descending," Hymnary.org, https://hymnary.org/hymn/CWH2021/487. Public domain (1758).
15. Augustine of Hippo, Quotes, Goodreads, www.goodreads .com/quotes/164594-in-my-deepest-wound-i-saw-your-glory -and-it.

CHAPTER 8: THE HOLY SPIRIT AND HEALING

1. I have adapted some of the material in this chapter from my book *The Unseen Real* (Franklin, TN: Seedbed, 2016), 122–24.
2. Raymond Brown, *The Gospel according to John, XIII–XXI* (Garden City, NY: Doubleday, 1970), 1139, emphasis added.
3. G. Campbell Morgan, *The Acts of the Apostles* (New York: Revell, 1924), 30–32.
4. John R. W. Stott, *The Message of Galatians* (London: InterVarsity Press, 1968), 148.
5. Gordon Fee, *Paul, the Spirit, and the People of God* (Peabody, MA: Hendrickson, 1996), 114.
6. Craig S. Keener, *Galatians* (Cambridge UK: Cambridge University Press, 2018), 260.
7. Thomas à Kempis, *The Imitation of Christ*, trans. E. M. Blaiklock (London: Hodder & Stoughton, 1979), 26.
8. Here are three books on spiritual gifts that I have found especially helpful: Kenneth C. Kinghorn, *The New Testament Gifts of the Holy Spirit* (Lexington, KY: Emeth, 2005); Sam Storms, *Understanding Spiritual Gifts: A Comprehensive Guide* (Grand Rapids: Zondervan Reflective, 2020); and C. Peter Wagner, *Your Spiritual Gifts Can Help Your Church Grow* (Grand Rapids: Chosen, 2017).
9. Kinghorn, *New Testament Gifts of the Holy Spirit*, 28–51. Used with permission.
10. Colin Gunton, *The Promise of the Trinity* (Edinburgh: T&T Clark, 1991), 37.

11. Quoted in John Akers, John Armstrong, and John Woodbridge, *This We Believe* (Grand Rapids: Zondervan, 2000), 147.
12. A. W. Tozer, *The Divine Conquest* (Old Tappan, NJ: Revell, 1950), 124 (emphasis original).
13. Richard J. Neuhaus, *Death on a Friday Afternoon* (New York: Basic Books, 2000), 90.